Resurrection Promises

**LEONARD H. BUDD
& ROGER H. TALBOTT**

*Sermons, Worship Resources, and Group Discussion
Questions for the EASTER SEASON*

C.S.S. Publishing Co., Inc.
Lima, Ohio

RESURRECTION PROMISES

Copyright © 1987 by
The C.S.S. Publishing Company, Inc.
Lima, Ohio

All rights reserved. No part of this publication may be reproduced, stored in a retrieval system, or transmitted in any form or by any means, electronic, mechanical, photocopying, recording, or otherwise, without the prior permission of the publisher. Inquiries should be addressed to: The C.S.S. Publishing Company, Inc., 628 South Main Street, Lima, Ohio 45804.

Library of Congress Cataloging-in-Publication Data

Budd, Leonard H., 1933-
  Resurrection promises.

  1. Jesus Christ — Resurrection. 2. Jesus Christ — Resurrection — Sermons. 3. Sermons, American. 4. Easter service. I. Talbott, Roger G., 1948- II. Title.
BT481.B68   1987   263'.93   86-28314
ISBN 0-89536-850-1

2.87 2T

7809 / ISBN 0-89536-850-1

Table of Contents

Foreword   9

Introduction   11

1. Resurrection: From Temporal to Eternal   13

2. Resurrection: From Chaos to Order   22

3. Resurrection: From Lesser to Higher Morality   32

4. Resurrection: From Sin to a Second Chance   42

5. Resurrection: From Burn-Out to New Vision   53

6. Resurrection: From Brokenness to Wholeness   66

7. Resurrection: From Slave to Child   75

About the Authors

Roger Talbott is minister of Chapel United Methodist Church in Madison, Ohio. He was associate minister at Lakewood United Methodist Church from 1981 to 1985, and also served United Methodist churches in western New York State. He is a graduate of Hartwick College and Colgate Rochester Divinity School. His wife, Jacquie, is an attorney. They have two sons, Matthew, 14, and James, 11.

Leonard H. Budd is pastor of the Lakewood United Methodist Church in Cleveland. His college and seminary training were at Ohio Wesleyan University and Oberlin, with studies for the Doctor of Ministry completed at the Methodist Theological School in Ohio. Previous to his current appointment he was pastor at Stow UMC and Wadsworth UMC, and has served as superintendent of the Wooster District of his denomination. He is married to Dr. Karen W. Budd of the Case Western Reserve University family. They are parents of two girls, Julie and Ellen. This is his third book published by C.S.S.

Every day is a personal Resurrection Day — sin is past, new body is risen to life, moving toward the life that is to be. Both are miracle: rebirth every day, rebirth to Life to Come.

Albert Schweitzer

Foreword

Two facts of our time are abundantly evident. One is the hunger for God under whatever name and in whatever way. Modern human beings express more of a God-hunger than we often recognize. Whether in splendidly ordered high church worship or in the swaying moans of sincere seekers after religious certainty, human beings, all over the world, hunger for God.

The second fact is the variety of ways in which this hunger is met. Some try to satisfy it by heavy emphasis upon spiritual healing, other by positive thinking, and still others by a highly intellectualized approach to a God whom they perceive as being too orderly for so much emotion.

With this kind of atmosphere, one welcomes the book, *Resurrection Promises,* by Leonard H. Budd and Roger G. Talbott. Here one finds a clear and moving account of the resurrection faith, complete with scriptures, pastoral prayers, and congregational responses. This kind of preaching is contextual in the best sense of that word. These are teaching sermons, of the type that speaks directly to the deepest hungers of the human heart. This volume is enhanced in many ways because it is the joint product of two pastors who have worked and preached together in a local church where the hunger for God can be satisfied in regular corporate worship.

I found *Resurrection Promises* to be strong and vital refreshment for my personal faith. It will be quite as helpful to lay persons in local churches as to pastor-preachers who need new light upon their way.

> James S. Thomas
> Bishop, Ohio East Area
> The United Methodist Church

Introduction

That glorious word from Easter, "He Lives!", is the Resurrection message that changed the world. The power of the Risen Christ proved that what had been seen as perishable was in fact enduring — what was temporal was now eternal. The Gospels tell the story.

Yet, the whole Bible message is a resurrection story. It begins with Genesis and comes to a life-saving conclusion with the affirmation of the disciples in the Garden and upon the Emmaus road. It is a message of God's eternal love, ever seeking to save, to hold, to redeem, to make free, to resurrect. That is the Bible story that begins in Genesis, and ends in the life that God has given each one of us. It is the story of God's resurrection power at work.

First is the glad shout from the Easter Day discovering that an empty tomb can mean a filled life. The seemingly perishable was enduring. The seemingly temporal was eternal (Chapter 1). Yet, to understand more fully the gift of Easter we venture back to the "beginnings" — even to Genesis. The event of creation, first pondered in times of pre-history, is a story of chaos being changed into order — and out of the order a faith. There is resurrection in that change (Chapter 2). The resurrection story moves to the developing moral order, framed by the Commandments. It marked the ancient Hebrews as different from their neighbors — a moral ascendancy was beginning (Chapter 3). The Bible story tells of a king discovering a resurrection from sin to a second chance. David found that in God's world a new beginning can be formed from a disastrous past (Chapter 4). Resurrection is seen in the prophet voice, spoken from the wilderness of Judea. That voice was first sounded in the cries of despair and defeat, but, with God's resurrection power, Elijah discovered new visions and a new life. He returned from the wilderness (Chapter 5).

St. Luke wrote of Jesus' gentle touch upon sightless eyes and upon twisted limbs. New ways of seeing brought resurrection to dark lives. Jesus' word allowed bent lives a new chance at "standing tall". It is miracle. It is resurrection (Chapter 6). Finally, the Apostle Paul, even as chains of iron hung loose upon his arms, told of slaves who were slaves no longer. Now, with the power of God in Christ Jesus, they were sons and daughters. The road he walked was like other roads — many other roads. One was the road from Bethany to Jerusalem. Those roadways bring one to the great affirmation that death is not the end of God's design. The Risen Lord overshadowed the experience of death. Those first disciples learned of Jesus' close presence — his resurrection presence and power (Chapter 7).

Thus we have come full-circle: The Bible's resurrection story from the proclamation of "He Lives!" through the many ways in which God gives life and back again to the new dawn of Easter's affirmation. That is the Bible's story. It is a story of hope that begins amid ashes and chaos — sin and brokenness — and ends with the bright light of God's Love giving a second chance, opening an Eternity.

Each chapter includes a story — mostly an imagined story — and some guidance for use both in a worship service setting and with small group discussions. This volume is dedicated to the members of The Lakewood United Methodist Church who first shared this resurrection journey in the early months of 1984.

Leonard H. Budd and Roger G. Talbott

Chapter One

Resurrection: Temporal to Eternal

Luke 24:13-35

*Almost two thousand years ago today
The stone upon His grave was rolled away,
And in the blinding darkness of the tomb
He rose and shattered there the grief and gloom
Within the hearts of those who worshiped Him.
Although that day and time have now grown dim,
One message through the ages has been hurled:
His love is hope and light for all the world.
And as the dawn of Easter fills the skies
We, too, with Him in spirit must arise;
For even underneath us in the earth
There is a faithful promise of rebirth.
If there's a stone against your heart today,
Look up to him and it will roll away.* *

The runner had stopped to catch his breath. He had covered almost three miles without letting up. Now he rested against a bent olive tree taking deep breaths that would bring strength to his tired muscles. He still had four miles to go, and he dared not stay too long, lest the great gates of the City be fastened shut — locking him out.

Despite his panting, and the pounding of his heart, the runner was joyous in the travel — elated beyond all his imaginations of past months. What he had heard earlier in the day, heard as mere dreaming by sad women, was now truth

---

*"Easter Message," by John Van Brakle, *Christ in Poetry*, edited by Thomas Curtis Clark, Association Press, New York, 1952.

to him. Christ was alive! Christ lived!

The runner turned toward the western horizon just in time to see the red ball of sun touch a hilltop. Soon darkness would envelop the land. And Jerusalem gate would be locked.

He began his run again, stretching each step to cover the miles. Now the running was a bit easier. The first miles from Emmaus had been on a small path, pocked with hooves of sheep, rutted by the quick running of rain water. But now he was on the main road, the high ridge road from the north that moved directly to the Damascus Gate of Jerusalem. This was the trade route, smoothed down by soldier legions and the thousands of pilgrims that streamed to the Hebrew capital with its Temple built by King Solomon. On this road the running was easier. It gave him time to think.

Just three days had passed since the horrible deed had been done. Their beloved Jesus had been snatched by betrayal, taken from prayer in the Garden and roughly hauled before one official after another. Finally, as tempers turned hot, and daylight creased the eastern sky, the order had been given by the Romans: "Crucifixion!"

"Can it be? Can it be that Jesus had done so evil a deed as to warrant Rome's worst? No!" The runner knew it was not so. His Master would not be traitor to the state or destroyer of the faith. Still, that had been the verdict. The punishment pounded crude iron nails into his hands and feet. The nails were longer than a man's hand span (nine inches) and the rough iron would have torn the skin and snapped the little bones and sinew. That crucifixion cross had been lifted into the sky. Jesus had hung upon it, strength seeping from his body with each breath. He was taunted by the robed priests. He was teased by the guards, and his last belongings scattered at his feet by the soldiers' right of conquest.

The painful memory came to the runner as he moved toward the city he had so recently left. Each dead tree, standing stark against the evening sky, was reminder to him of the cross that had held Jesus' body in place until a merciful death was achieved.

Shortly thereafter, with gentle but hurrying hands, Jesus' body was eased down from the cross. Since the Hebrew Sabbath was about to begin, his wounded body was hastily wrapped in a cloth and carried into the tomb lent by Joseph of Arimathea (Matthew 27:57). There the once vibrant Nazarene was laid out on a slab of stone. His body was still, cold. As the sundown came, the tomb was sealed with a large stone rolled into place before the door. The words remembered then were the final words Jesus had spoken. In the pain and humiliation of his last hour, Jesus had said, "It is finished."

What was left? Nothing! The dream of God's Kingdom was broken and cast aside, even as were the bones scattered upon Golgatha. The gladness of the teaching time was now only fading memory. The intimate fellowship of love and compassion and concern was now impossible — for there, beyond the stone doorway, lay the dead body. Nothing was left. Truly, it was finished.

The runner remembered it all as he made his way along the ridge road to the City. Jesus had implied such an end, telling his close disciples of the troubles that awaited even as thy lounged about the table Thursday evening. That sweet communion of souls had been a blessed time — a time of rememberance strangely interlaced with sadness. Never again would it be the same. Never again would Jesus be so near. Never again would his word of blessing seem to make everything so right. "It is gone, for certain. It is finished!"

It was that sad, sad finality that had led the runner and a companion to leave the city earlier this very day. "Why stay here?" was their early morning question. "There is nothing left for us in the fellowship. There is nothing left but memories that bring hot tears."

As they made the final farewells, even then the woman's word was coming back. As the two bid their last good-byes the woman had run in with the tale of meeting Jesus again, a story of an empty tomb. But such is meaningless talk — mere wishful dreaming from mistaken conversations with a gardener. "Do not play with our emotions, woman! Jesus is dead. You yourself laid his body on the stone." In just such fashion the two men had spoken to the women and then made their way out of Damascus Gate, walking with slowed feet north along the ridge road and then westward to Emmaus.

Once more the runner stopped to catch his breath. It was getting darker now, with only a distant line of the city wall visible. He knew now that he would be late. The gate would be closed and locked. He was too late for sure.

Breathing hard and fast, he began the running again. He was spurred on by the later remembrances. Toward noon he and his companion had just been saying, "It is too late" (meaning the death of Jesus), when a third person had joined them. They had not seen his approach, but there he was, cloaked tight and walking in step with them. Hesitant at first, the two entered into cautious conversation, commenting on the weather, the road conditions. Only later did they talk of what hung most heavily upon their hearts. But the stranger seemed not to know. "You must be the only one in all Jerusalem not to know of Jesus' death!" they told him. It began for them a recounting of ministry, of deeds and words, that suddenly brought Jesus close. Their pace picked up, and the invitation was extended, "Would you sup with us? Break bread with us this night?" The stranger accepted. In that meal together, in the village of Emmaus, seven miles from the Holy City, as the afternoon sun slipped to the horizon, it was known to the two that the stranger was no stranger (Luke 24:13-35).

They did not perceive it instantly, but it did not matter. "Did not our hearts and souls catch fire as we talked?", they said. "It was Jesus with us. The women were right. The Master *is* alive. The Christ *is* risen. We know it. He was there! Did you see the way the bread was broken and shared. Just as before. And the words spoken. They were the teachings." That moment came back in quick remembrances. It was for them, the resurrection of Jesus Christ from the dead. In those moments they understood that God's work begun in Christ would not be ended. New hopes continued, even as in Galilee; Christ was near, close.

And now the runner was approaching the high, dark Jerusalem wall, outlined by watch-fires here and there. Damascus gate was shut tight. The sentries were guarding from the top. The runner shouted up, "I must enter — it is life and death." The guard, looking at the runner's sweating body reflected in the fire light, saw his intensity and the obvious exertion of the run.

With a wave of his hand he directed the runner to seek the maze gate, a little portal with a zig-zag passage way through which one man at a time might fit. It was so tiny some called it the "needles's eye way." With difficulty the runner found the opening and shouted through. "I must enter the city." From the other side a rough guard voice called out questions, seeking name and residence and reason. The runner answered, "It is a matter of life. The news I have. They await my word." After considerable delay, and further questions, the runner was admitted. He carefully inched through the narrow, twisting opening.

Through the deserted streets of the city the runner made a difficult way. In the darkness many turns were wrong and he had to retrace his steps. But on he went until he found the steps leading to that upper room. The door was fastened. He could hear voices inside — familiar voices. His knocking on the door brought a sudden silence inside. He knocked again. Still silence. Finally he shouted out his name, and the fact of his run from Emmaus.

It was Simon Peter who came to the door, calling his name through the wood, carefully unlatching the ties. The door opened very slowly and the runner pushed his way in — shouting the news even before fully in the room. "We broke bread with Christ. He lives!"

THE STORY OF THE RUNNER is, of course, imagined. It grows from the Easter account of the two disciples who met their Risen Lord on the road to Emmaus. It is an account fround in the 24th chapter of Luke's Gospel. In this imagining no names were used because I want the runner's name to be *your* name. Indeed, you are the runner — you who claim Christ as Lord and Saviour.

The Easter affirmation discovered long ago is the same affirmation known today: The temporal things of earth turn to dust, they fade with time and disappear. Yet, through God the power of Jesus Christ overcame death and opened Eternal dimensions.

Easter is not the empty tomb — it is the new awareness of God's power. Easter is not burial cloths — it is a sense of communion with Christ and one another in the Love of Christ. Easter is not angels — it is the knowledge for me and you that Christ Jesus *is* alive, because God's power for life is stronger than earth's power of death.

That message, spoken for more than 1,900 Easters, is the power of Faith. With the Faith, that believe, nothing on earth has greater power. The Apostle write, "Death, where is thy sting!" Christians through all the ages have affirmed his word, that in the love of God nothing can touch us — not even earth's death. No wonder they shouted "Hallelujah! Hallelujah!" Their shout is ours as well! "Hallelujah. For the Lord God Omnipotent reigneth!"

Worship Aids for Easter Day

Easter Scripture Reading

The Witness from St. Matthew (28:1-6):
Now after the sabbath, toward the dawn of the first day of the week, Mary Magdalene and the other Mary went to see the sepulcher. And behold, there was a great earthquake; for an angel of the Lord descended from heaven and came and rolled back the stone, and sat upon it. His appearance was like lightning, and his raiment white as snow. And for fear of him the guards trembled and became like dead men. But the angel said to the women, "Do not be afraid, for I know that you seek Jesus who was crucified. He is not here; for he has risen as he said."

Congregational Response:
Praise God for a resurrection faith that sees Christ Jesus free of the tomb.

The Witness from St. Mark (16:5-7):
And entering the tomb, they saw a young man sitting on the right side, dressed in a white robe; and they were amazed. And he said to them, "Do not be amazed; you seek Jesus of Nazareth, who was crucified. He has risen, he is not here, see the place where they laid him."

Congregational Response:
Praise God for a resurrection faith bringing hope to a lost humanity.

The Witness from St. Luke (24:5-9):
And as they were frightened and bowed their faces to the ground, the men said to them, "Why do you seek the living among the dead? Remember how he told you while he was still in Galilee, that the son of man must be delivered into the hands of sinful men, and be crucified, and on the third day rise." And they remembered his words, and returning from the tomb they told all this to the eleven and to all the rest.

Congregational Response:
Praise God for a resurrection faith to share, bringing new life to a sinful world.

The Witness from St. John (20:19-20):
On the evening of that day, the first day of the week, with the doors shut where the disciples were, for fear of the Jews, Jesus came and stood among them and said to them, "Peace be with you." When he had said this, he showed them his hands and his side. Then the disciples were glad when they saw the Lord. Jesus said to them again, "Peace be with you. As the Father has sent me, even so I send you."

Congregational Response:
   Praise God for a resurrection faith that brings Christ Jesus close to us all, empowering us in the hope of life eternal. Alleluia! Amen!

Easter Pastoral Prayer
   The rock is rolled away! The death-tomb is empty! See, the embalmer's cloths now lie limp upon the ground. The word is spreading. The hope is articulated from mouth to ear to mind and heart. Christ is Risen! Death has no power over him! Easter light shines abroad!
   The mystery of Your ancient work, O Resurrection God, is still shadowed upon the mind, yet the heart tells the story. We do not have all the answers of Your freedom from earthly-powers. Yet we know enough to see the change that worked upon Your ancient disciples. Their cowardice was transformed into power. Their question into belief. Their earth-born life into heaven-bound existence.
   But we live with mystery all the time. How do airplanes fly? How does electricity flow? How does love begin? And in the mystery of life we find life. So it is for Easter and our living.
   We, too, would give praise that earth does not have the final word.
   We, too, would lift a glad shout that death is not the sudden end.
   We, too, would know the ancient's exultation that resurrection life flows through us all.
   O, Resurrection God, spirit creative, bless us with that Easter Life finding our completeness in a living untied to earth's rocks and caves, but tied to Your ever-living Son, Jesus Christ our Lord. Amen

Study Suggestions for Chapter One

Group Builder

In a small group, ask each person to describe a time when he or she was the bearer of good news. This may have been the announcement of a child's birth, telling someone that he or she qualified for a promotion or new job, awarding a prize, letting someone in trouble know that help would be coming, or any other form of good news.

Discussion Questions

1. The author begins with a graphic description of the crucifixion of Jesus. Why is it necessary to understand the crucifixion in order to understand the resurrection?

2. Evangelism is often thought of as "telling" the Good News of Christ to someone. Many evangelists insist that evangelism begins with listening to people. In the light of your answers to question 1, and in your own experience of telling people other kinds of good news, what should you listen for before you tell another person about Christ?

3. Read Luke 24:13-35 and discuss:

    a. How did the Stranger prepare the disciples' hearts to understand the good news of the resurrection? How does Christ work in people's hearts today to prepare them to receive the good news?

    b. When were their eyes opened to see that the Stranger was Christ? Do you believe that people have personal encounters with Christ today? Is such a personal encounter necessary in order to be a Christian?

4. Halford Luccock has written, "Good news cannot walk. It runs." What factors make the telling of the Easter story urgent in our world today?

Chapter Two

Resurrection: From Chaos to Order

Genesis 1:1-31
Hebrews 1:1-4

The fire was beginning to die. With a simple wave of his hand the Ancient One sent the young boy racing back into the scrubby land to fetch sticks for burning. Overhead the moon lit his path as he ran from one thicket to another, pulling together the loose twigs and picking up a stray dry root. Quickly he returned, throwing the meager kindling on the dying fire. In the short span of minutes since his hunt began the Ancient One had fallen asleep, his head dipping down to his chest. With the crackling of the new twigs he came alive and picked up the beat of his story.

"Long ago, beyond the time of all our ancestors, back before the sun and moon were put into the sky," he said, "back when everything was chaos, God formed the world." The Ancient One was speaking words he had long ago heard from another Ancient One. The words, exact phrases remembered, were the literature of those long ago people. It was before the time of writing. We call it "pre-history." But there *was* history, for there were human lives moving upon the face of the earth. And those human lives asked questions, and pondered answers. Those human lives, beginning in the fertile crescent of land at the eastern edge of the Mediterranean Sea, were the first — or at least part of the first. And in those dawny-days of humanity they asked deep questions, and pondered even deeper answers.

The story that the Ancient One spoke to the young boy on this evening was the story of creation. "How did it all come to be?" That was the question asked in that dim long ago. Those human beings felt the warmth of the sun in day. They knew the cold of the desert night. They saw the variety of life that came and went, that seemed to follow some plan of motion — even as the sun moved silently across the blue sky. These early, early human lives saw the hunted as animal stalked animal. They share in it, stalking prey that provided them with food and clothing. They saw their own lives grow through cycles that brought them to the mystery when life ceased and the body returned to the dust of earth. There seemed an order. Yet, even as the boy and the Ancient One sat by the fire, there was the possibility that a wild animal would devour them both — even as the fire continued. Life had uncertainty. They sought to answer the unknown, thereby making it the known.

It was an age before the pyramids. It was a time before the Babylonians built an empire, or even before the ancient Ur was hometown of Abraham. It was before the flood that marked so many cultures of old. It was back at the beginning, and they talked of the beginning. It marked a unique understanding, an understanding that continues to affect us today. Its root is pre-history. Its fruition is even shaping twentieth century people. The story is of a Plan, a Mind that willed Order from Chaos.

The Ancient One told it again so that it would not be forgotten. He told it because it was answer to the pondering. It was an answer that shaped a faith about life. It made him comfortable as he sat by the fire, and it gave security to the young man growing up in that so long ago. And it still is a foundation stone of faith, our faith, a faith that can neither be proven, nor disproven.

Stirring the burning twigs, the Ancient One began again to speak the story. It came word for word as he had received it. "In the beginning God created the heavens and the earth. The earth was without form and void, and darkness was upon the face of the deep; and the Spirit of God was moving over the face of the waters. And God said, 'Let there be light.' And there was light." (Genesis 1:1-2)

OUR BIBLE BEGINS with the story of Creation. It is the first of the Bible's many resurrection stories. Actually, the Bible begins with two creation stories — one in the first chapter and the second in the next chapter. Both stories, coming to us from those very earliest of speculation about life, grew from the belief that life was orderly, was following a plan, was fulfilling the destiny of a great mind.

Of course, it was shaped in days long before speculation could be examined with microscope or telescope. The word spoken by that Ancient One to the young lad was of a creation that brought order from disorder. It was of a creation of purposefulness and progression. It was an act of ancient faith, but it gave comfort and surety. Yet what is it for us? We live in a world of scientific speculation and proofs. Does an ancient story have acceptance? Can it have meaning? Has the Ancient One's word been superceded by the scientist's laboratory?

Science tells us of the "Big Bang" theory of creation — with a moment some 15 to 20 billion years ago when a giant fireball exploded. The shrapnel of that explosion is still flying outward. Some of the fragments are the Milky Way, one of the hundreds of billions of stars is the earth's sun, with its tiny orbiting grains of planets.

In our century that theory has been supported first in 1913 by Astronomer Vesto Slipher of Lowell Observatory in Flagstaff, Arizona. He discovered galaxies receding from the earth at extraordinarily high speeds — up to two million miles per hour. Then, in 1929, American astronomer Edwin Hubble developed findings to formulate his law of an expanding universe that presupposed a single primordial explosion.

Finally, in 1965, two scientists of Bell Telephone Laboratories (Arno Penzias and Robert Wilson) picked up the noise of background radiation coming from all parts of the sky. What they were hearing, it turned out, were the reverberations left over from that first explosion, the hissing echoes of creation. It is awesome!

But does it forever wipe away all earlier speculations? All ancient faiths?

Harvey Tananbaum, an X-ray astronomer at the Harvard-Smithsonian Astrophysical Laboratory, says: "That first instant of Creation is not relevant as long as we do not have the laws to begin to understand it. It is a question for philosophers and religionists, not for scientists."

Robert Jastrow, when with NASA's Goddard Institute of Space Studies, wrote: "With the Big Bang theory, science has proved that the world came into being as a result of forces that seem forever beyond the power of scientific description." The primordial fireball of Creation blocks everything that was before it. Temperature of the universe in the first seconds of its existence was many trillion degrees. What was left was a dense fog of radiation. Said another scientist: "The first million years are as concealed from us as the face of God."

Biologist George Beadle, formerly president of the University of Chicago, spoke this affirmation:

> *In early Biblical times . . . it was believed as a matter of faith that man was created man. Since then, science has led us back through a sequence of evolutionary events in such a way that there is no logical place to stop . . . until we come to a primeval universe made of hydrogen. But then we ask, "Whence came the hydrogen?" and science has no answer. Is it any less awe-inspiring to conceive of a universe created of hydrogen with the capacity to evolve into man than it is to accept the creation of man as man? I believe not!**

Beadle is a respected scientist speaking in the same tones of

---

*Time magazine, February 5, 1979, p. 149.

awe and wonder as did the Ancient One to the little boy.

And it is a tenet of Christian faith, shared from the beginnings of human thought and meditation, that beyond and before Creation is God. The intent of God holds the process for Order and Reason and Purpose. It is not observed under laboratory microscopes, but it is felt in the heart, and held in the Spirit's abode.

Another story, this one true. Perhaps it brings us full circle. It is the story of a modern Ancient One. Emile Cailliet was professor of Christian Philosophy at Princeton Theological Seminary.** Philosophers are modern-day Ancient Ones! They deal with ideas that seek to bring light to mystery, and order to the unordered. Emile Cailliet was brought up in the French intellectual community at the turn of this century. It was a society rooted deeply in naturalism — total reliance on the tenets of physical science.

Cailliet served in World War I, saw friends killed by random bullets and was wounded himself. In these growing years — even as he hunkered down in a foxhole — he longed for a philosophy, a "believing," that would — as he put it — "understand me." He tried to write it out through his own journalizing — noting down his thoughts and meditations day after day. Surely, he thought, these meditations on rereading would speak to his own personal condition, his questions, his needs. On a beautiful sunny day he sat under a tree, opened his book of notations, and read with growing disappointment. It would not work. It was of his own doing. It carried no strength, no persuasion.

Was it coincidence? On returning home that day his wife presented him with a Bible. As hard as it is to believe, it was the first time that Emile Cailliet held a Bible in his hands. He began to read it. He continued to read it. "I could not find words to express my awe and wonder. And suddenly the realization dawned upon me: This was the [word] that would

---

**Emile Cailliet, *Journey Into Light,* Zondervan Publishing House, Grand Rapids, MI.

understand me . . . I continued to read deeply into the night
. . . And lo and behold! the One of whom they spoke, the One
who spoke and acted through the Bible, came alive to me. The
God of Creation was revealed in the Love of Jesus Christ.

His life changed and grew. He came to this country and
knew a brilliant career as teacher, a Christian philosopher at
Princeton University. Through the experience of being in‑
troduced to Jesus in the French Bible, Cailliet found the an‑
swers to questions that had gone unanswered for so long. He
discovered and order amid disorder, a Reason with a capital
R. In Jesus he found the personification of the Mind of Crea‑
tion — of God.

THERE ARE MANY forms of knowing. Science is one. So
are experience, and intuition, and faith. Science proceeds on
the theory tht there is a discoverable answer to all mystery
— and the discovery comes about step by step. Faith, by defi‑
nition, is a leap to gain answers to the mystery.

I propose a belief, shaped by such a leap of faith, that the
full circle is made:

Creation words, spoken by the Ancient One to the little
boy by the kindling fire, talked of a genesis, a beginning planned
by God.

Science words spoken by scholars confess that science can
push back just so far; beyond that is still mystery.

Professorial words found through Faith in God a quality
of living that gives purpose and order.

The full circle, I believe, is that all three words grow from
one great word. And that one great word is the very start of
the Bible's resurrection journey. It is the tenet of faith from
which the resurrection powers of life emerge. That great word:
"In the beginning, God . . ."

Everything that follows is but amplification, refinement,
clarity to a deeper and broader knowledge. "In the beginning,
God . . ."

Worship Aids

Call to Worship:
The Psalmist calls us to worship: Sing to the Lord a new song ... Sing to the Lord, bless God's name; tell of God's salvation from day to day.

Opening Prayer:
O Master of the multitude,
    Toilworn, dust-stained, and tanned,
The rich and poor, refined and rude,
    Of every time and land —
Come, walk with us and talk with us,
    And share our grief and woe;
O Master of the multitude,
    Teach us thy love to know.*

Hymn Response:
"At Thy Feet, Our God and Father" (v. 1)

Continuing Prayer:
O Master of the multitude,
    The millions wander still
Without a guide, without a light,
    Without an aim or will —
Come walk with us and talk with us
    Among our people move;
O Master of the multitude,
    Redeem us by thy love.*

Hymn Response:
"At Thy Feet, Our God and Father" (v. 3)

The Pastoral Prayer
O Lord Jesus Christ, you taught us to pray. Yet we confess that we have not used this great resource nearly enough in our lives. We have time to worry, but we do not have time to pray about our troubles. We have time to read the paper and watch the news and complain about the government and the communists and the economy;

---

*Chauncey R. Piety, *Worship Resources for the Christian Year,* edited by Charles L. Wallis, Harper & Brothers, New York City, 1954. Used by permission.

but we do not have time to pray for our leaders, for our enemies, or for the world. We have time to make lists of things to do and we even have time to pursue projects which seem to have no meaning or purpose; but we do not have time to begin our days with the searching examination of prayer.

O Lord Jesus, you taught us to pray, yet we confess that we have not used this great resource. We do not now want to waste any more time in useless self-recrimination. We know how we are when we forget that we are living in your presence. But now in this moment we know that you are with us. We know we no longer have to carry our burdens alone. In this time of prayer each of us can reach into the bag of worries that we carry around with us and take them out one-by-one and place them into your hands. And so we do that now, O God.

We put our worries about death in your hands.
Our worries about money.
Our worries about our families.
Our worries about our jobs.
Our worries about our relationships.
Our worries about our souls.

And as small and weak and as powerless as we seem in the world's eye, O Lord, we know that we wield in this time of prayer the greatest power in the universe. We swing a sword that beats all the other swords into plow shares. We carry a scepter that the Lords of the earth must obey. We have a wealth worth more than all the gold and silver in the world. We unite our hearts with your heart, we unite our wills with your will, we unite our spirit with your Holy Spirit. Amen

The Benediction

The Psalmist sends us upon our ways: Declare God's glory among the nations, his marvelous works among all the people. Amen

Study Suggestions for Chapter Two

Group Builder

Ask each person to respond to the following questions:

1. Where do you come from? What was your birthplace?

2. Each of us has probably said to ourself: "If I only knew then what I know now..." What is one truth you have learned in life that you wish you could pass on to someone younger than yourself?

3. When or where or how did your faith-journey begin? Were you influenced by a person? Did it begin in a certain church or community? Did it begin with an experience that caused you to question and search?

If you choose to use this group builder, point out at the end that all three answers given by each person are different ways of answering the question "Where did you come from?" — answers on the levels of fact, experience, and faith.

Discussion Questions

1. Many people see a conflict between the scientific and Biblical understanding of the origin of the world. How does the author suggest that science and faith reinforce each other? In what ways do you personally believe that science and faith conflict or reinforce each other?

2. The author says that the main point of the Biblical story of Creation is that God has brought order out of chaos. Why did ancient people believe this? Why do some modern scientists believe this? Why did Emile Cailliet believe it? Can you think of other ways God has brought order out of chaos in your life or in our world?

3. Ancient people experienced order in the changing seasons and chaos in an unexpected attack by an animal. How do modern people experience order and chaos in their lives? How does faith help people deal with chaos?

Chapter Three

Resurrection: From Lesser to Higher Morality

Deuteronomy 51:1-22
Matthew 5:17-48

Sarah was five years old. She had lived all her life in a little village in Galilee, six miles from the shore of the great Sea. She had never been farther away than the olive tree grove, a long stone's throw from the last house of the small community. But then, Sarah was only five. She lived with her grandfather who was unofficial rabbi for the twenty families of the village. Her grandfather, by his knowledge of the scripture, was the source for understanding the Hebrew law.

Sarah's town was distant from the many Jewish fishing villages that rested against the great Sea of Galilee. The nearest to her was Capernaum. But had Sarah gone in the opposite direction, walking not to the Sea, but walking away, up the sloping roads that eventually led to Mount Herman, she would have come to the foreign villages. These were communities of people not Hebrew, people who followed different gods, who lived in different ways. Her grandfather had told Sarah, and everyone else in the village, "Never walk to the north for that is an unclean place. Never go up toward the mountain for you will meet people who live differently. They are bad. They are evil."

At age five, Sarah did not understand all that was meant

in her grandfather's prohibition. She could not understand the cultural differences that had produced varied ways of living. She did not even understand about different gods, and differing moralities that grew from different gods. She only knew that she must never walk north — uphill — for that was to the foreign villages. And so that she would never accidentally make that journey, she never went any direction away from the village. She only went as far as the olive trees on the road toward Capernaum.

Sarah and her grandfather and the people of the village lived in the days of Roman rule. It had been 187 years since the Maccabean revolt in Jerusalem (167 B.C.). That is the way they calculated time — if they ever bothered much with time. We would call it the year A.D. 20. It was the year 20 after the understood birth of Jesus. And even as Sarah was living in the little village six miles away from Capernaum, Jesus was growing up in Nazareth, some twenty-five miles southeast of Capernaum.

The respect that Sarah's grandfather had with the village people grew from his knowledge of the Law. He read with great reverence the early books of scripture, the first five books of our Bible. From these ancient writings the people of the Hebrews drew their "life qualities." The law, or Pentateuch, shared the story of the beginnings — including the gift of Law from God, a gift that came dramatically through Moses and the Ten Commandments. From these rules of behavior and respect to God the people of the Hebrews had developed an elaborate code of conduct. It was a morality that marked them very different from their neighbors. Part of that difference was in the grandfather's warning to never, never associate with the foreigners. In such a touch might come a spiritual contamination that would weaken the moral standing of the community.

And it *was* different! The moral standing of the Hebrews was what we would call an "advancement" over the peoples that surrounded them. The laws of the Hebrews often set a greater value on human life than on animal life. Even in the practices of slavery, the Hebrews practiced a humane conduct. The Law said,

> When you buy a Hebrew slave, he shall serve six years, and in the seventh he shall go out free, for nothing.
>
> (Exodus 21:3)

No neighboring culture held slaves so highly. The ancient Hebrews practiced punishments of "a life for a life." Other cultures might kill a whole village in retaliation for a single death.

And the Hebrews recognized a special moral tie to God. God gave them the law. Had not Moses received it directly on the mountain top? Therefore, when a person offended the society by breaking the Law, it was also an offense against God (1 Samuel 12:9-10). The Hebrews recognized community responsibilities — often making the judgment as one extended family when a judgment was called for (Exodus 21:22-23).

Indeed, as Sarah's grandfather told the little village the law, he taught that the morality of life — the following of the law — was the central way in which God was honored. He would say, "When you refrain from stealing, you thus honor the Almighty God. When you give honor to your parents, God is honored. When you do no murder, you thus pay respect for the life God has given.

So you see, the growing morality within Judaism, separating them from the foreign peoples around them, became a growing mark of its uniqueness. They were the people of the Law. That meant a respected quality to living.

Ten years passed. Ten years further from the Maccabean revolt in Jerusalem. Now it is the year A.D. 30 by our calendars. Sarah is fifteen years old. Her grandfather, following a short illness in which the whole village cared for him, had died and was buried on the south corner of the village — that corner closest to Jerusalem. It had been his fondest wish to visit the holy city before his death, but that was not to be. Instead, his body now rested in the village earth nearest that most holy site.

At fifteen, Sarah is on her own. That is not unusual. As the village is an extended family, she is cared for by others and contributes her share into the work of planting and harvesting, into the herding, into the making of the olive oil and the weaving of cloth from the sheep's wool. She is busy, as are all the women of the village.

Within the busyness one day there came an interruption. It was first seen as if a conquering army was stirring the road dust out of Capernaum. Sarah was the first to see it. She was at the olive grove harvesting and turned to see a cloud of dust, and then the people causing it. She ran back to the village to alert the elders. By the time all were assembled, the distant people were close. It was a joyous throng, pressing close to the young, bearded man who was obviously the leader. As they entered the center of the village, the elders walked cautiously forward to meet the smiling leader. He quickly shouted, "Peace to you all. God's blessing rest here." He looked around as he spoke. His smile and words, and the countenance of the crowd that followed him, proved their friendly intent.

Before half a day had passed, the leader — Jesus of Nazareth — had won the hearts of all the villagers. He talked with the little children and the old widows. He was interested in their ideas, their problems, their life. He even fixed a wooden table, saying that he was trained as a carpenter. Throughout his visiting he spoke of God as his Heavenly Father. There was such a familiarity to his words that the people uncounsciously looked around to see of the Heavenly Father was not somehow standing nearby, even as an earthly father might proudly stand near his son.

In his time in the village Jesus proved that he knew the law even as Sarah's grandfather had known it. He could speak verses of the ancient codes. He could tell stories of the ancient history. He could pull from his memory just the proper phrase of Law to answer a timid or confusing question.

Yet, there was something new. The Law that Sarah's grandfather taught was of outward acts; very stern. Somehow the Law that Jesus discussed ended touching inward feelings. Years later Sarah still could remember, word for word, Jesus' teaching:

> You have heard that it was said to the men of old, "You shall not kill; and whoever kills shall be liable to judgment." But I say to you that everyone who is angry with his brother shall be liable to the judgment.
>
> (Matthew 5:21)

Jesus also said:

> You have heard that it was said, "You shall love your neighbor and hate your enemy." But I say to you, Love your enemies and pray for those who persecute you, so that you may be [children] of your Father who is in heaven . . . For if you love those who love you, what reward have you?
>
> (Matthew 5:43)

Sarah and the village people listened intently to this new rabbi from Nazareth. They had known from their earlier learnings that the Law was a great gift from God, and morality in life was a strength for good. They had known their own morality to be stronger and higher than those around them in the foreign villages. But now Jesus was teaching something new — a morality more inward than they had known before. It was a morality that affected the mind as well as the act, the will as well as the doing.

Before leaving the village in mid-afternoon, Jesus had said, "Think not that I have come to abolish the Law and the prophets; I have come to fulfill them!" Sarah remembered that so very well for it was the keystone of decisions that she was making within her own mind and heart that day. In talking of the laws the people loved, Jesus had claimed a way that would lead to completing them. Sarah remembered.

In talking with some of Jesus' close followers it was noted that they, too, lived by a code of conduct that was most honorable and respected. Their hearts were as their deeds.

Now we hurry on with the story. Ten more years pass. Sarah is twenty-five years of age, married and the mother of three children. Her husband is the village carpenter. They are happy in their life together, and within the village. Not many in that village have forgotten the day when Jesus first visited the town. He had returned three other times — and then he was gone. Word had come back some months later that Jesus had gone to Jerusalem. In confrontation with the Chief Priest and other learned-ones, he had taught as he had done so often in their village. But in Jerusalem it had brought about his death. He was nailed to a Roman cross.

Yet even as that word was cried upon the village streets, another word followed. It was a word of mystery; yet not so mysterious to those who had really known Jesus. "He lives," was the first of the new word, shouted by a boy who had run all the way from Capernaum. "He lives. He is not dead." The village people did not see Jesus again with their own eyes — but they were one in their assurance that he did truly live. And he lived for Sarah's three children, too, and others who were yet unborn.

To the village people, part of Jesus' aliveness was the morality they practiced, the ethics of right and wrong, good and bad, honest and dishonest. It was known as far away as Capernaum — and perhaps farther — that because of Jesus' teaching the people of the village were good people, people to be trusted.

THERE IS, within the Bible tradition, a "new birth" in moral life. It is a resurrection that marks the followers as different from the non-follower. The morality of human behavior began to be charted in very ancient days, but it was not a static thing. It grew as did the species. But it has grown no higher than the example of Jesus. The world is still working to attain it. As it does that work, new resurrections of life are achieved.

There is a modern, funny story that goes like this: A man consulted a psychiatrist. He complained, "I've been misbehaving, Doc, and my conscience is troubling me." The doctor asked, "And you want something that will strengthen your willpower?" The fellow replied, "Well, no, I was thinking of something that would weaken my conscience."

Sarah would not have laughed at such a story, for the weakening of conscience would not have been something she would have wanted. Sarah, in the time between her fifteenth year and her twenty-fifth, had become a follower of Jesus. In that following she strove for a new morality, a new strength of doing the right and shunning the wrong. Because she was a disciple of Jesus, his influence for ethical living was resurrected in her life, and her ethical living was resurrected in the life of her three children, and in their children, and on and on it goes.

Worship Aids for Easter 3

Call to Worship
This is the day which the Lord has made... this day, these hours. Let us rejoice and be glad in it. Let us know the happiness of discipleship and the freedom of God's forgiveness and care. Let us worship God, and praise God for Jesus the Christ.

Opening Prayer
No pictured likeness of my Lord have I;
He carved no record of his ministry
   On wood or stone.
He left no sculptured tomb nor parchment dim,
But trusted for all memory of him
   Human hearts alone.*

Hymn Response
"Blessed Jesus, at Thy Word" (v. 1)

Continuing Prayer
Who sees the face but sees in part;
Who reads the spirit which it hides, see all;
   He needs no more. Thy grace —
Thy life in my life, Lord, give thou to me;
And then, in truth, I may forever see
   My Master's face.*

Hymn Response
"Blessed Jesus, at Thy Word" (v. 3)

The Pastoral Prayer
Eternal God, it is a hard direction that we must be perfect (Matthew 5:48). It is understandable that the hearing of the word would drive us to our knees, heads bowed in fervent prayer, for we cannot be perfect. We can only strive toward it. Is that what your Son meant? Is that what You intended for your human creation — that we always strive toward perfection?
So it is that as a congregation we pray, first asking your forgiveness, for in the days past we have been far from perfect. There have been words uttered from our mouths that should never have been

---
*William Hurd Hillyer, *Worship Resources for the Christian Year*, # 102, edited by Charles L. Wallis, Harper & Brothers, New York City, 1954.

said. And, Gracious God, we are guilty of deeds done that should never have been done; things that we have contributed to, things that we have given our voice to, things that should not have been done. We pray for your forgiveness. And, in ways known only to You, and to the deep recesses of our own hearts, there are words we did not say and things we did not do that our striving for perfection should have voiced and should have accomplished. For our sins of omission we ask your forgiveness.

But, with forgiveness received, we then, O God, know the power that can come for you as we move out on this "first day of the week". You, O God, would be part of the words that we do speak in the days ahead, and in the deeds that we do. You would be part of our life, O God, blessing that life, encouraging that life even as you forgive that life.

So it is that we hear these ancient words from Your ever-living Son, and we would know again the possiblities of good life that rests with us, a life intended by you for us. Amen

Benediction

This is the Day which the Lord has made . . . this day, these hours. Let us now depart in the knowledge of God's love, in the protection of God's caring, in the power to live for Christ Jesus, our Lord and Saviour. Amen

Study Suggestions for Chapter Three

Group Builder

In a small group ask each person: When you were a child, what was one rule that your family had that made you different from some of your friends? (Examples: Clean your plate. Call adults "Sir" or "Ma'am". Be home early.)

Discussion Questions

1. In what ways did the Old Testament law make the Jews different from their neighbors?

2. In what ways did Jesus and his teachings seem different to Sarah from the morality of the Jewish law?

3. Ask someone to read Matthew 5:21-22 and Matthew 5:27-28. Why do you think that Jesus placed such an emphasis on inner thoughts and feelings? Is it possible to live by such morality? How would your community be different if everyone lived by this morality?

4. Read Matthew 5:43-44. Can you think of examples of individuals or groups who lived by this morality? What are the barriers to living by this morality? In what ways do our fears get in the way of loving our enemies?

5. Why would the resurrection of Jesus allow people to live by a higher morality?

Chapter Four

Resurrection: From Sin to a Second Chance

Psalm 23
2 Samuel 12:15b-25
1 Peter 2:21-25

The afternoon sun was waning as the shepherd boy, David, led his sheep down the well-worn path that led from the green pastures to the pool of still water where his flock would quench their thirst before heading back to the fold. He glanced back at the flock following him; then stopped and looked more closely. Where was Ayin, his big ram? One of the lambs was gone, too. The shepherd boy shaded his eyes against the late afternoon sun. In the distance he saw the big ram lumbering down the hill along a different path, the little lamb following behind.

"Something has caught Ayin's eye," the shepherd boy thought. He shouted at the sheep, but they could not, or would not, hear him.

The boy couldn't leave the rest of his flock to go after them. He marked Ayin's direction in his mind and then hurried off to get the others watered and into the fold for the night.

The shepherd boy picked up the trail of his lost sheep at dusk. His experience told him the direction they would take. Tufts of wool left on briars and ominous drops of blood were left along the path. The drops became a steady trickle leading to a ravine that the shepherds called "The Valley of the Shadow," because it was so steep and deep that even at midday the sun did not penetrate to the bottom of the narrow gorge. As darkness fell the shepherd boy started into the Valley of the Shadow.

Years later David walked again in the afternoon sun; but he was no longer a boy; he was a man. He was no longer a shepherd; he was a king. He was no longer on a hillside outside of Bethlehem. He was on top of a palace in Jerusalem. Escaping the heat late in the day, he looked out over the city. He saw a woman bathing. Marking the house, he inquired who lived there. One of his soldiers, he was told. A brave man named Uriah who was helping lay siege to the Ammonite city of Rabbah. The woman must be his young wife, Bathsheba.

David told his servants that he wished to meet Bathsheba — tonight.

As a shepherd boy, David followed a sheep straying from the path. As a king, David strayed from the path of righteousness himself. It is so easy to stray from the path. If it could happen to the composer of the twenty-third psalm, it could happen to anyone. It usually does. As the prophet Isaiah said, "We all, like sheep, have gone astray, each of us has turned to his own way." Peter puts it more strongly, "You were continually straying like sheep." When that happens, we become as lost as the shepherd boy's big ram and small lamb.

As a shepherd boy David entered the Valley of the Shadow as one who was searching. As a king, he was not the one who was searching but the one who was lost. The valley was not a ravine near Bethlehem, but a state of mind and heart that one can experience anywhere.

David was in the valley of the shadow of self-deception. Perhaps it began when he did not lead his army off to war. He may have claimed that he was too busy attending to the affairs of state to fight his own battles anymore. Busyness is the best excuse for laziness. Maybe he told himself that he was beyond temptation when he invited Bathsheba to his house.

Maybe he told himself that what happened between them was all Bathsheba's fault. And maybe later, when he tried to cover up Bathsheba's pregnancy, he may have persuaded himself that he was doing her husband a favor bringing him home from the front; giving him a chance to go home and spend the night with his wife. When Uriah failed to take advantage of the opportunity David may have felt the he was justified in eliminating Bathsheba's husband. David may even have congratulated himself that he found a way for Uriah to die in battle; allowing the wretch to die like a hero. Maybe David even believed that no one would notice that Bathsheba delivered her baby too soon after their wedding and too long after Uriah had gone off to war.

WE WALK IN THE VALLEY of the shadow of self-deception when we start lying to ourselves. One of the most effective lies begins with the words, "At least I'm not . . ."

Perhaps David said to himself, "I may be an adulterer, but at least I'm not the kind of man who just uses a woman and then discards her. I may have arranged for Uriah's death in battle, but at least I'm not a cold-blooded murderer."

We need to be aware of the "at-least-I'm-not" game right now while we listen to David's story. It is easy for any of us to say, "I may not be a saint, but at least I'm not an adulterer like David." Or, "Maybe I have jumped some fences in my time, but at least I've never killed anybody — at least not like David did."

We enter the valley of the shadow of self-deception whenever we believe that what the Bible says about sin somehow doesn't apply to us.

St. John says, "If we claim to be without sin, we deceive ourselves and the truth is not in us."

Being human, we go astray and enter the valley of the shadow of self-deception all the time, and we cannot get out unless someone rescues us.

That is what the shepherd boy intended to do for his lost

sheep. As he entered the Valley of the Shadow, he checked the heavy, weighted rod at his belt. If he needed a weapon in this darkness, his sling would be of little use. He felt his way through the dark ravine with his staff. He no longer needed the trail-signs to guide him for he could hear Ayin's frightened bleating and the lamb's weaker cry. The shepherd boy knew that the sound of his voice would frighten the big ram, so he reached out with the crook of his staff and caught Ayin around the neck turning him around. Then holding Ayin securely the boy felt for the lamb. The baby was to weak to walk so the shepherd boy lifted the lamb to his shoulders and driving Ayin ahead of him with his staff, they made their way out of the Valley of the Shadow.

The Lord came looking for King David in the Valley of the Shadow, too. Nathan the prophet was the staff God used to get David turned around and drive him out into the light.

The Lord's staff is the staff of truth. Sometimes however, we cannot even see the truth unless it comes to us first in disguise, approaches us in the dark and takes us by surprise. Nathan came to David like a prosecutor comes before a judge. He told David about a poor man who had only one sheep which he had raised as a family pet. The poor man's children had played with the sheep, and the animal had been fed from their table. One day, their neighbor, a rich man with large flocks, took the poor man's one sheep and killed it, serving it to a visitor.

King David, the former shepherd boy, was indignant. He was incensed. He demanded to know the rich man's name so that he could be punished. Nathan said simply, "That man is you."

It was here that the staff of God shot out and turned David around. The truth hit him and he saw himself for what he was. He quit saying, "At least I'm not . . ." and started saying, "My God, I am . . ."

Jesus reaches out with the staff of truth when he says, "Judge not lest ye be judged . . ." "Don't try to take the speck out of your brother's eye, when you have a two-by-four in your own." "The measure you give will be the measure you get." In other words, it so often happens that the very thing we are most insistent that we are not is the very thing that we are.

We may have said over and over again, "At least I'm not . . ." one thing or another. Then the staff of truth turns us around and we say, "My God, I am . . ."

It is painful to be wrenched around like that. It is painful to finally admit:

"My God, I am an alcoholic, after all."

"My God, I am a racist, after all."

"My God, I am self-destructive, after all."

"My God, I do think and act and talk like an atheist about 90% of the time, after all."

"My God, I am unfair."

"My God, I am unfeeling."

"My God, I am everything I have always hated in other people and said I would never be."

It is painful, but only the staff of truth can turn us around and get us out of the valley of the shadow of self-deception, and into the light where, sadly, we often are met with the rod of despair.

It is this rod that the shepherd boy took from his belt that night he brought Ayin and the lamb out of the Valley of the Shadow and into the moonlight. He laid the lamb on the ground and carefully examined it. The lamb had suffered terribly for innocently following the big ram. Perhaps the lamb might live a little longer, thought the boy. But he knew by looking at the lamb's injuries that it would only be a matter of days before he was pushed out of the flock and the wolves finished him off. Days that the lamb would live in pain and fear. Ayin nudged the little animal and bleated pleadingly at David the shepherd boy, but the shepherd saw what the sheep could not see. The shepherd knew what the sheep could not know. The shepherd made a decision that the sheep could never understand. The shepherd raised his rod and brought it down on the lamb's skull.

Perhaps it was his memory and his conviction that the Lord was his shepherd that enabled David to face the rod of despair. The rod of despair hits when you realize that you have done something terrible that you can never undo. Had David only taken a sheep from Uriah, he could have restored it a hundredfold. But David could not give back to Uriah his wife or his life.

Probably all of us know something of David's feelings in that moment. You know that there are words which, once said, can never be unsaid. There are confidences which once broken, can never be restored. There are injuries which, once inflicted, can never be healed. If you have ever said one of those words, broken one of those confidences, or inflicted one of those injuries, you know exactly how David felt. You wish to God you could go back in time just one minute or just one day to stop whatever was about to happen; but you can't.

What do you do when you are hit by the rod of despair? You do what David did. You leave it to God to sort out. You accept the consequences. You hope for the resurrection.

David and Bathsheba's first child died. I do not know why. I do not believe that God demands the death of a child in payment for a parent's sin. I do believe that the Good Shepherd sees what we cannot see; knows what we cannot know; and sometimes makes decisions we will never understand as long as we live.

David was forgiven. David went on living. I do not understand that either. He certainly didn't deserve it.

Then I think of that shepherd boy and his straying ram who caused the death of the little lamb. I can see the boy in my mind's eye turning from the little lamb he had to kill and in fury raising the rod over the big ram's head; then catching himself at the last moment with the thought that Ayin didn't know what he was doing. And I see the shepherd boy taking the big ram by the horn and leading him back to the fold. I see the shepherd laying out grain for Ayin as one sets a table. I see him anointing Ayin's head with oil to heal the cuts and bruises. I see him pouring water into a big cup until it runs over and giving it to the sheep to drink. And I see time passing, another spring returns. A new little lamb chases after Ayin.

And we read that David, hearing of the child's death, got up, took a bath, covered his body with lotions, put on clean clothes, and went to pray in the house of the Lord. He came back again and ate, and then went in to comfort Bathsheba. In due time, they had another son, Solomon.

There is good news here for all sinners. It is the good news of the second chance. Even if you and I stray into the Valley of the Shadow, God does not abandon us. God is with us. God's rod and staff comfort us with an almost terrifying love. There may be pain, but there is also healing, renewal, and most important, a second chance.

God picks up the pieces of our shattered lives, often rearranging them, and hands this new life back to us. So we say with David, "Surely goodness and mercy shall follow me all the days of my life."

That is the good news for the sinner, but is there any good news for those who are sinned against? Any good news for Uriah or for the baby that died? If the story ended here there would be none.

The story doesn't end here. It doesn't end with the birth of new lambs in springtime nor the birth of David and Bathsheba's son. It goes on through Solomon's son and through his son — through the generations until a son is born at the end of David's line who is also God's son. He, too, was like an innocent lamb led to the slaughter. He, too, was wounded for our transgressions. He, too, died when those who deserved to die went on living and were given a second chance — but he also rose from the dead.

We believe that the resurrection says that there is hope, not only for the sinner, but also for those who are sinned against. There is a second chance not only for those that go on living, but also for those whose lives have been destroyed by sin. We believe that the resurrection means that someday all the tangled messes that we have made in life will be straightened out. Righteousness will be restored, and we will dwell in the house of the Lord, forever.

Worship Aids for Easter 4

Call to Worship
"He maketh me to lie down in green pastures, He leadeth me beside the still waters, He restoreth my soul. He leadeth me in the paths of righteousness for His name's sake." (Psalm 23) Let us lay down our burdens and worship God. Let us have our souls restored by the still waters of the spirit, So that we may walk in the paths of righteousness for sake of Christ.

Opening Prayer
He built no temple, yet the farthest sea
Can yield no shore that's barren of His place
    For bended knee.
He wrote no book, and yet His words and prayer
Are intimate on many myrid tongues,
    Are counsel everywhere.*

Hymn Response
"O Jesus, I Have Promised" (v. 2)

Continuing Prayer
The life He lived has never been assailed,
Nor any precept, as He lived it, yet
    Has ever failed.
He built no kingdom, yet a King from youth
He reigned, is reigning yet; they call His realm
    The kingdom of the Truth.*

Hymn Response
"O Jesus, I Have Promised" (v. 3)

Pastoral Prayer
O Lord, our Shepherd, you sent your son Jesus Christ to look for your lost sheep, for those who had strayed from the path of righteousness. The best of all good shepherds even gave his life for his sheep. Therefore, we know that we can bring to you all the problems that sin cause in our lives.

---

*Therese Lindsey, *Christ in Poetry*, p. 89, edited by Thomas Curtis Clark, Association Press, New York City, 1952.

We bring to you the problem of shame. We have learned to be ashamed of what we have done, and said and thought. We are even ashamed of things that have been done to us. Like Adam and Eve, we try to hide our shame. We try to cover ourselves so that other people, and you, and even ourselves, will not see.

As we bow in prayer, we sense that you are all-knowing. You know all desires. From you no secrets are hid. Yet, this cross above our heads reminds us that you love us more that we love ourselves. You accepted us. You have chosen to carry our shame. Beneath the cross we bow, and offer thanksgiving.

We remember in our prayer that sin not only causes shame, it also causes pain. We have hurt others, O God; we have injured the innocent. We have said things that cannot be unsaid. We have done things that cannot be undone. Yet, beneath the cross we know that you chose to take all the pain upon yourself. You chose to forgive. Beneath this cross we give thanksgiving.

We remember in our prayer that sin disrupts your divine plan. Even though you will that we should have everything we need, sin causes some to starve for lack of bread or lack of love. Even though you have willed that we should live in harmony, sisters and brothers together, sin breaks that possibility. Even though you have willed that we live in perfect trust and obedience, sin fills us with fear and causes us to seek security in false gods.

Yet, we bow in prayer beneath the cross, remembering that your Son has determined to straighten out the mess sin has made of our world. It was He who broke the bread, shared the love, created the harmony, and took away the fear. Therefore, always, we give thanks in prayer and praise His name. Amen

Benediction

Now may the Lord spread a table before you, even in the presence of your enemies. May the Lord anoint your head with oil. May your cup overflow, Surely goodness and mercy shall follow you all the days of your life. And you will dwell in the house of the Lord forever. Amen

Study Suggestions for Chapter Four

Group Builder

Ask each person to share briefly an experience of being lost and being "rescued" by someone else. This may be a childhood experience or a recent one. It may be the experience of literally being lost in an unfamiliar place or the experience of feeling lost in a new and difficult situation. Emphasize that they are to share experiences of being helped by others, rather than a time when they found their own way out.

Discussion Questions

1. David's sin was dramatic, but what are some of the less dramatic and more universal ways in which people "stray from the path" of the Bible's message?

2. Discuss the implications of this statement: "We tend to judge others by their actions, yet judge ourselves by our intentions!"

3. Seek to define the meaning of the theological words "sin" and "redemption". (Perhaps a book of theological definitions would be helpful.) How are these ideas part of our religious life today?

4. Compare your definitions of "sin" and "redemption" to the stories you shared about being "lost" and "found". In what ways is sin like being lost? In what way is redemption like being found? How has God come looking for us?

5. The sermon raises the question of why the innocent suffer for the sins of others. Can you describe specific circumstances in which the innocent often suffer for the sins of others? Can you think of specific times when mercy has been shown to the undeserving? In what ways does the crucifixion and resurrection of Jesus offer help and hope to both the undeserving and the innocent?

Chapter Five

Resurrection: From Burn-Out to New Vision

1 Kings 19:1-18
Matthew 11:25-30

Elijah's feet pounded on the trail. His legs stretched out to cover the miles. He outran the king's chariot. He outran the wind blowing up the storm-clouds overhead. Strength to run like this after the day he had been through was a gift from God.

God had been giving him strength like that all along; strength that had always amazed him. There had been the strength to tell King Ahab that he was a fool and a blasphemer. There had been the strength to prophesy that there would be no more rain until Israel called again on the name of the Lord. On this very day God had given him the strength to win the most dramatic contest the world had ever seen.

The terms of the contest had been simple. In the presence of the people of Israel, both the prophets of Baal and the prophet of the Lord were to build altars to their respective gods, lay firewood beneath a sacrfice, and implore their god to light the fire. Four hundred fifty prophets of Baal, shouting and blowing horns, had failed to rouse their god to action. Elijah, on the other hand, brought down fire from heaven with a simple quiet prayer. Fire that consumed not only his sacrifice but the stones of the altar.

Elijah then rallied the Israelites to slaughter the prophets of Baal. Next, with another quiet prayer from Elijah, a cloud no bigger than a man's hand appeared in the western sky. The wind began to blow and the cloud grew and darkened and Elijah commanded the king and his people to hurry home before the storm struck.

Finally, as the first drops of blessed rain began to fall on the parched earth, Elijah ran up the road toward the royal city of Jezreel. Ahab, had left Mt. Carmel before Elijah, but with the miraculous strength from the Lord Elijah outran the king's chariot. Elijah would be standing in front of Ahab's house to show the king that he could not escape God.

THE STORY OF ELIJAH'S CONTEST with the prophets of Baal impresses me deeply everytime I hear it. Yet I admit that I cannot readily identify with it. Calling down fire from heaven is out of my line.

On the other hand, I can identify with Elijah the runner. Elijah is always on the move. Elijah is always running from one thing to another, and so am I, and so are many of you. Running is part of the modern life-style. We run to work. We run to the store. We run to night school. We run to meetings. Those of us who have children in school find ourselves running to lessons, to dentists, and to athletic events. Those who have older relatives find yourselves running in to check on them; running to the doctor or to the nursing home.

It is not surprising that all this running tends to burn us out. "Burn-out" is mental, emotional, physical, and spiritual exhaustion. There is an epidemic of burn-out in our society. Some dismiss this saying that burn-out has become stylish. I'll admit that in some circles I run in, you have to at least pretend to be burned-out or people will think you are not a responsible adult.

Setting aside our pretensions of busyness, I would say that most of the problems that I encounter as a pastor on a daily basis are related to tiredness. People are simply burned-out from running from one responsibility to another. It may do us good to learn that Elijah experienced this profound tiredness, too. Within days after his great victory on Mt. Carmel, Elijah felt totally defeated. The man who had run like the wind reached a point where he could hardly stand up. The man who had been the center of attention of an entire nation, felt miserably lonely. The man who had communicated with God on the mountain top, felt far away from God in the valley. The man who had called down fire from heaven, was totally burned-out himself. Elijah burned-out when he quit running on faith and began running on fear.

Whether you think of yourself as a person of faith or not, there have been times in your life when you have run on faith, just as Elijah did in his contest with the prophets of Baal. Like Elijah, you have had days when you have run on a strength that surprised you.

Sometimes it is the strength to care for a sick loved one for days or weeks or months.

Sometimes it is the strength to get through a funeral.

Sometimes it is the strength to say what ought to be said.

Sometimes it is the strength to keep quiet.

Sometimes it is the strength to survive a terribly painful situation.

I'm sure you must have had times in you life that you look back at with no less wonder that Elijah must have looked at that twenty mile run from Mt. Carmel to Jezreel. You wonder, "How did I do that?" The only answer that any honest person can give is, "I must have been given a strength beyond my own."

As we look at those situations in which we ran on a strength beyond our own, we see that the distinctive quality of this strength was courage; especially the courage to love when loving was difficult and the courage to do what was right even when it would have been easier not to do it. After we were through exercising this courage we may have been very tired. We may have needed rest; but we did not have that burned out feeling of loneliness, spiritual depletion, and total exhaustion. These were the characteristics of the burn-out Elijah experienced when he stopped running on faith and began running on fear.

The day after his victory on Mt. Carmel, Jezebel vowed to do to Elijah what Elijah had done to the prophets of Baal. So we read that Elijah ran. He ran for his life. He ran from the hills of northern Israel to the desert valleys of the Negev, a distance of 100 miles.

This run is out of character for Elijah. He had to run and hide at other times in his life, but he always did it at the direction of the Lord. There is no word from the Lord in this run; only Elijah's fear. It is somewhat reassuring to know that even someone as faithful as Elijah could sometimes get so caught up in his running that he didn't take time to stop and listen to God.

We see that Elijah could run pretty far on fear and so can we. Fear is a powerful motivator. Some people think it is the only motivator. Some bosses think people only work when they are afraid. Many of us think that we do our best work under pressure. Therefore, we arrange our lives in such a way that we are always racing deadlines. Or we create images of failure in our minds in order to arouse the fears that will pump the adrenaline that will get us going. Sometimes we raise this to a religion. We imagine a judgmental God who stands over us with a check-list of things He expects us to accomplish in our lifetimes and we'll be damned if we don't get them done.

It is good for us to know that we were not meant to run on fear. This is the real point of that famous story about Mary and Martha. When Jesus praised Mary for sitting and listening while her sister was in the kitchen getting dinner, he did not condemn Martha for working. He simply said, "Martha, Martha, you are worried and anxious about so many things." In other words, "Martha, you are running on your nerves. You are running on your fears." Jesus was not saying contemplation is better than activity. No one was more active than Jesus. No one accomplished more in less time than Jesus did.

Like Elijah, Jesus was always on the run. But Jesus always ran on faith, never on fear. The issue for him was not the running, but what he was running on.

We see the effect that running on fear had on Elijah. First, there is a terrible exhaustion. At the end of this hundred mile run into the desert, Elijah sat under a broom tree and prayed that he would die. Not all of you will understand that prayer, but some of you will. You know what it is like to be so tired that you envy the folks who are on their way to the cemetery. You literally wish you could lie down and sleep forever. Or, if you haven't reached that extreme, you may have fantasized about being sick. Maybe you have thought how nice it would be to have some kind of painless illness that was nevertheless so serious that your physician would order you to go to the hospital and stay in bed until she tells you that you can get up.

We see another symptom of burn-out when Elijah says, "Lord, take my life; for I am no better than my ancestor." What he means is that on a scale of ten his self-esteem is at minus five. One of the main symptoms of burn-out, besides exhaustion, is feeling rotten about yourself. It often happens to people who, like Elijah, have spent their lives trying to do their best. Often we start out running on faith striving to reach some high ideals. Then, because we are afraid of being less than responsible or less than loving, we start running on fear. Our ideals become tyrants that are always judging us, making us feel like failures because we can never live up to them. We become more and more exhausted, less and less able to live up to our ideals, and thus we feel worse and worse about ourselves. It is a vicious cycle that leads us to think in the end that we are worthless human beings.

When we are burned-out we feel terribly lonely. Elijah says to God, "I have worked so hard for you, and what has it amounted to? Nobody appreciates what I have done. Nothing has really changed. I'm all alone in this. No one is helping me." The burned-out have a difficult time getting help. They are too afraid to stop running. They have too low an opinion of themselves to think that anyone would want to help them. They may even become paranoid, seeing enemies that aren't there.

Burn-out is a kind of spiritual death. The miracle is that anyone is ever resurrected from it. Yet scattered among you are many who could testify to the fact that people do rise out of it. If burn-out is one of the most common spiritual ailments in our modern world then the resurrection from burn-out is one of the most common experiences of God's grace that our world has.

In this story we see how the graciousness of God saves Elijah's burned-out body, mind, and spirit.

First, there is the grace of limits. There may be no limit to what we can do by faith. Faith may be able to move mountains. There is, however, a limit to what we can do when we are running on fear. Elijah could run like the wind on faith. When he was running on fear, he reached a point where he had to stop. God had built limits into Elijah's body.

Your body, too, has limits. Most people encounter these limits sooner or later in life. Some learn to read the physical and mental signs that are like the warning lights on the dashboard of a car. Since we don't have an owner's manual for our bodies we have to figure out those signs for ourselves. For some, it may be a sore throat or a vague ache or pain. For others, the sign may be a tendency to snap at people or an inability to concentrate. The list goes on. However, when we are really running on fear, we tend to ignore these warning signs and keep on driving ourselves until we burn-out our engines.

Not every serious illness can be blamed on running on fear, but many of them are at least partially caused by this tendency to push ourselves. As many of you have learned, a serious illness — even a heart attack or a serious emotional breakdown can sometimes be a friend if it teaches us the graciousness of the limits God has given us. One hard-driving executive continued to wear his hospital bracelet after going back to work following a mild heart attack as a continual reminder that he had limits.

Sometimes the only way the Good Shepherd can make us lie down in green pastures is to wait until we drop from exhaustion. Then the Good Shepherd can lead us beside the still waters and restore our souls.

God restored Elijah's soul by waiting until Elijah dropped in the desert after running too far on fear. The Lord let Elijah sleep. Then an angel awakened Elijah and gave him something to eat.

Being spoon fed by an angel may sound a little bizarre, but it shows us that resurrection from burn-out does include physical resurrection. Ultimately all food and all healing come from God, though farmers and grocers, doctors and nurses may be the angels that convey these things to us.

However physical resurrection is not enough. We are not healed of burn-out when a doctor says we can go home. Nor are we preventing burn-out just by eating right and keeping physically fit. We must turn away from the fears that led to burn-out and turn toward God. The biggest problem with running on fear is that it seems so hard to find faith again.

When we want to find a new relationship with God we would do well to follow Elijah's example. Elijah found his faith again by returning to his religious roots. He went back to the place where his religion was born. He journeyed to Mt. Horeb, better known as Mt. Sinai, where hundreds of years earlier, God had given the ten commandments to the people of Israel. He followed the example of the greatest person of faith he could think of, Moses.

Sometimes we need to make a mental and spiritual pilgrimage back to the roots of our faith. During the Middle Ages, those charged with the cure of souls often prescribed pilgrimages for burned-out Christians. They were told to go back to some holy place where people before them had found faith. Sometimes a personal pilgrimage does help. One of this century's greatest missionaries, E. Stanley Jones, made a habit of returning from time to time to his home church and kneeling at the altar where he had first given his life to Christ. A pilgrimage can mean returning to some disciplines of worship; a time of private prayer each day and going to church on Sunday. John Wesley and other early Methodists made an intense study of the gospels to discover what it was that gave those early Christians such a strong, dynamic and joyful faith. Always, for Christians, it means going back to Jesus.

Often in going back to the roots of our religion we find a new, stronger faith than the one we had before.

It is an experience that is somewhat like that of a married couple who go on a second honeymoon hoping to recapture the passion that brought them together in the first place. They discover, not the old passion, but a new love. The years that they have shared together, and the people they have become in each other's company have given them new and deeper reasons to love each other; reasons the younger, less mature people they once were would never understand.

In going back to his religious roots, Elijah found God in a new way. Elijah climbed Mt. Horeb and he learned in prayer that the Lord's presence would come to him. Then a mighty wind shook the mountain, but the Lord was not in the wind. Then there was a fire, but the Lord was not in the fire. Then there was an earthquake, but the Lord was not in the earthquake. Finally, there was a still, small voice.
God had spoken to Elijah in the storm, but not today.
God had spoken to Elijah in the fire, but not today.
God had spoken to Elijah in earthshaking miracles, but not today.

God would speak to Elijah in a new way, a quieter way, a way that would require Elijah to stop and listen before he started running again.

We need to stop and listen before we start running again. Go back to the roots of your faith and really search for God. Remember the Scriptures:

"All who seek me shall surely find me."

"Draw near to God and God will draw near to you."

"Be still and know that I am God."

God will speak. God will re-establish a relationship with you. It will be a new relationship; different from and deeper than the relationship you may have had earlier in life.

But the re-establishment of your faith is not the end of the story. God not only restored Elijah's faith with the still, small voice. God also restored Elijah's vision. By that I mean that the Lord changed the way Elijah looked at himself and God.

He saw, first of all, that God still had plans for him. That he wasn't useless. We often need that restoration of vision when we are burned out. We need the reassurance that we have value and that life isn't over.

Secondly, Elijah saw that the success of those plans depended on God, not on him. To be sure, God would use Elijah. All of Elijah's effort would be required, yet God and not Elijah would be responsible for the outcome. That, too, is something we need to know when we are running on fear. We think we are responsible for things over which we have no control: for the way our children will turn out, for the health of our loved ones, for the success of our church, for the fate of the world. We have an important role to play in all of these things perhaps, but we are not in control of the ultimate results. We are, in some ways, like an assembly-line worker who makes one weld in one part of an automobile. We are not asked to lie awake at night worrying about the design of the car. We are not asked to constantly run up and down the line making sure that everyone else is doing his or her job. We are called to be faithful to one task. For most of us that means just being ourselves and doing what God has placed in our hands this day as faithfully as we can.

Finally, Elijah's eyes were opened to the fact that he was not alone:

"There are yet 7,000 in Israel who have not bowed the knee to Baal," the Lord told Elijah.

This may be the greatest act of grace and the one that keeps restoring our faith and keeps us going without burning-out. It is the knowledge that there are other people out there who believe what we believe and feel what we feel; people who share our faith, our hopes and dreams, and who know what it is like to live by them and even what it is like to fall from them and to rise again.

That is why I thank God for Elijah. I do not know what it is like to call down fire from heaven. I do know what it is like to be always on the run. I know what it is like to run on faith. I also know what it is like to run on fear. I know what it is like to feel burned-out. I also know what it is like to rise out of ashes of burn-out with a renewed faith and hope — a new relationship with God — a new appreciation of God's plan for me and for other people. In Elijah I find a kindred spirit, just as I have found in many of you. That is why we need these Bible-people. That is why we need each other. That is why we need Christ himself, for he became like us and he understands what it is like to run through life. Amen

Worship Aids for Easter 5

Call to Worship
The question is asked: What does the Lord require? The answer is given in Scripture words: To do justice, to love mercy, and to walk humbly with God. (Micah 6:6-8) Guided now by those words, and faith in the truth of those words, we begin an hour of worship.

Opening Prayer
Judean hills are holy,
    Judean fields are fair,
For one can find the footprints
    Of Jesus everywhere.
His trails are on the hillsides
    And down the dales and deeps;
He walks the high horizons
    Where vesper silence sleeps
One finds them in the twilight
    Beneath the singing sky,
Where shepherds watched in wonder
    White planets wheeling by.*

Hymn Response
"O Sabbath Rest by Galilee" (v. 3)

Continuing Prayer
He haunts the lowly highways
    Where human hopes have trod
The Via Dolorosa
    Up to the heart of God.
He looms, a lonely figure,
    Along the fringe of night,
As lonely as a cedar
    Against the lonely light.
Judean hills are holy,
    Judean fields are fair,
For one can find the footprints
    Of Jesus everywhere.*

---

*William L. Stidger, *Christ in Poetry*, page 248, edited by Thomas Curtis Clark, Association Press, New York, 1952.

Hymn Response
"O Sabbath Rest of Galilee" (v. 4)

Pastoral Prayer
Eternal God, your spiritual guidance has come to us in many ways. There are commandments and parables and wise, wise sayings. There is preaching and example, words and deeds. We do thank you for all the guiding that is provided — even if we turn our backs to it or shut our eyes.

The laws of the ancient ones guide us. We are thankful for the "thou shalt" and the "thou shalt not" that form patterns of right and wrong. Without the guiding of that moral road map we would stumble and fall — indeed, life would be very terrible. Even if our wills are not up to it, our minds tells us that life is better when framed by the Commandments. Forgive our childish neglect of them; support our growing use of them.

The human family, created by you, O God, to be in communion with you and with one another, is guide to us. We are helped by one another: encouraged, befriended, healed, made whole. We dare not shut the windows of life, cutting off our ties to those around us. You have made us, Eternal God, to be a family-being. Here, in this gathering at worship, we are sustained. Our spirits are nourished. We pray for the abilities to care for one another.

Even as the prophet of old found that "still, small voice within," so we would be hushed to listen and to respond. You do not shout at us. You only speak in ways that need our attentive hearts. We listen now. Speak to us, O God, and guide the steps we take. May right be done, and wrong be shunned. Speak to us, O God, the message of your Son, our Lord. Amen

Benediction
Depart now in the presence of the Holy Spirit; strengthened by God's power, enlightened by Christ's teaching, enriched by Spirit gifts, and comforted by the holy presence of God. Amen

Study Suggestions for Chapter Five

Group Builder

Ask each person to respond briefly to the question, "If you could go back to a place where you once felt close to God, where would it be?" (A person who cannot remember being close to God may be able to identify a place where he or she felt inspired, or experienced inner peace.)

Discussion Questions

1. Illustrate from personal experience the difference between "running on faith" and "running on fear." How does a person move from fear to faith?

2. On a blackboard or newsprint, list at least five different things that God did to restore Elijah's faith after he was burned-out.

3. On a blackboard or newsprint, list at least seven kinds of people in your church or community whom you feel susceptible to being burned-out by their jobs or family responsibilities. Be sure to include volunteer postions in your church that tend to burn people out.

4. Looking at the first list you made, how does God use your church to provide physical or spiritual restoration to burned-out people? In what ways could your church become a more effective instrument of restoration? You may develop some practical suggestions that should be presented to your church's leadership. Be careful that your expectations do not burn them out!

5. For group sharing or private reflection: Look at the list of the ways in which God restored Elijah. Which specific thing would be most helpful to you right now in restoring your strength or faith for daily living? Close by praying for each other.

Chapter Six

Resurrection: From Brokenness to Wholeness

Matthew 15:29-39

His name was Jahmai. In the ancient lineage of his people Jahmai was one of the sons of Tola (1 Chronicles 7:2), a worthy man and father of a great tribe by the days of King David. But the Jahmai of our story lived much, much later in the Hebrew lineage and his grand namesake was long forgotten. The Jahmai of our story was a youth, and this day he walked behind the crowds that followed Jesus. His walking was slowed because of his left leg being bent, never going straight. It meant that he would step-slide, step-slide, step-slide where others would step-step. For as long as he could remember, and that went back most all his fourteen years, he was the last to arrive any place. Other children his age could run ahead and be the first. Jahmai was always the last.

And here he was again, following the people out of the town, last in line as the procession came to an open area of high grass. Jahmai knew that his leg would always limit him. He knew that forever he would be not quite right, hindered from the sort of completeness that other children knew. His mother had simply raised her eyes heavenward when asked about it. There was no answer. The hard delivery that she had known with Jahmai was long-since forgotten as other children were born. The pulling of the little baby legs, the hurry to complete the birth, the cries — all were forgotten. So when the question was asked, "Why, Mother is my leg so twisted?"

she could only raise her eyes to heaven. There was no answer. Yet, there was the ever-present question, "Why?".

This day, this hot summer day, it seemed that half the village was gathered around Jesus. That was why they had moved from the pounded ground of the village center to the grassy area beyond the last village house. More space was needed for the teaching time. Walking the short Sabbath Day's distance to the outskirts of the village would allow all the people to hear Jesus, and even sit in the cool grass. Most were already positioned, pressing close to the seated Jesus, as Jahmai with his step-slide arrived.

Jesus had often been to the village, on the edge of the Galilee Sea. From those waters the village people drew their life. The men fished during the night. Lantern lights fastened to the boat prows attracted the fish into the nets. With the first light of day, the boats would head for the rocky shore line. The whole village would meet them to sort the fish, to mend the nets, and to listen to the men tell of the night's adventure upon that sea so easily roughed by the winds from Mount Herman.

Jahmai, except for his leg, would have been trained to fish the waters. But his unsteady stance would have put himself and others in peril. So Jahmai was told to stay upon the shore, and be of help to those who stayed behind, those who waited for the fisherman to return. How much his life was chained to his leg, that crooked leg.

Jahmai had often heard of Jesus' wonder with healing — the power that he had to heal sick bodies. There was that young girl who everyone knew was dead, yet with Jesus' touch she lived. There was the old woman at Peter's house in Capernaum who was so sick she could not rise from her bed. But with Jesus' words she was made well. There was the report that had swept back to the community that a man's blindness was changed to sight. And that a woman's constant bleeding was healed. Jahmai knew that even within his own village people had been brought to Jesus, carried miles and miles, in order that Jesus might simply touch them — or that they might reach out and touch the hem of his cloak. They knew, and Jahmai believed it too, that with just a touch all would be right. Life would be whole. Pain would be gone.

Jahmai could not help thinking, "But what about me? What about my crooked leg?"

Jesus was now teaching. It was more like a gentle intermingling conversation. His words flowed freely meeting questions that poured from the people. Jesus' wisdom was not the scroll-learning that was so often voiced in the synagogue. Jesus' wisdom came from somewhere else. He certainly knew the sacred scrolls. He could recall the history of God's people as surely as the rabbi, but there was a warmth, a personalness to his teaching. Almost, it seemed, as if he had always known the answers, had always been shaped by the ancient teachings. Almost as if he were the teaching!

This particular day, seated in the cool grass of the field, and feeling more than ever the hurt of his physical limitation, Jahmai ventured a question himself. With a boldness he did not know he had, the youth called out, "Jesus, Jesus, can you help me walk?" Jesus turned, searching out the voices, the young voice. "Who called me?" he responded. "Where are you?" Others near Jahmai turned in his direction and helped to point out the boy who now stood with his hand raised. "I am Jahmai from the village." "Come here," Jesus called. "Come to where I am."

Jahmai moved with his usual step-slide gait through a thin path that was now opened by the crows. As he made his way along, there was no doubt as to the problem. That little bent leg tagging behind, an appendage of little use when compared to the many strong and athletic youth of the village, Jahmai stood before Jesus. His eyes were fixed upon the man, eyes that were partly fear-filled, partly hope-filled, and partly resigned to his fate. Jahmai had hoped so long and so hard and with so little result that he dared not now cast too great a hope upon the moment.

Jesus looked down to the bent leg, and stooped down to

touch the twisted knee. "My friend," he said, "life is not just arms and legs — nor eyes, nor ears. Life, my friend, in all its forms is a gift from God, blessed by God." Jahmai stood still. He did not understand. He only knew that Jesus had touched his knee and nothing had happened.

"Your name is Jahmai?" Jesus continued to talk with him, not conscious of the crowd that was now hushed in anticipation. "That is a great name, Jahmai. One of our forefathers was named Jahmai. Grandson of Issachar. Son of Tola. A great tribe of our people."

The youthful Jahmai, from a distant, foggy teaching in the synagogue remembered the name — but nothing more. Jesus continued, "And it means something special, Jahmai. It means 'God keeps, God guards.' Did you know that, Jahmai? Did you know that God keeps you? God guards you?" Jahmai did not know. He only wondered in those moments why Jesus told him those things — why he told him those things as he stood balanced on his one good leg.

"Jahmai, let me tell you of Peter," Jesus continued. "See him there, resting against that tree? Just yesterday Peter lacked a faith in the care of God — such a faith that he could have moved through a stormy sea as our boat was offshore of our town. Peter saw all the waves about him, and he saw the storm clouds above him, and he said to himself, 'I can't!' And he began to sink deeper."

Two other disciples, listening to the conversation nodded agreement and smiled in the remembrance.

"But I am not afraid of the waters, Jesus." Jahmai was getting bolder. "I would *like* to be a fisherman on the sea." Jesus smiled at Jahmai's reply, recognizing that only part of his message was understood. "It was not the sea, it was the lack of faith in God's care. Peter, too, is a fisherman. But he was thinking only of the 'cannots'. He was concerned only with the bad, the frightful. He did not understand the good, the possible — even the miracle."

Jahmai looked down at the twisted leg, the bowed out

knee. He was silent, thinking deep thoughts. "Can it be that God does care for me?"

Jesus, with his calloused carpenter hand upon Jahmai's shoulder, turned more to the crowds and spoke now in their direction. His words taught that life is more than body, more than clothing, more than numbers of years. Life, as God has given life, can be rich by strengths of faith that grow from belief in a caring Heavenly Father. Some things are not possible in God's world, but so much more is possible. In the care of God, what might be hindrance can, instead, be means of learning, means of growth, means of resurrection to something new. God keeps his creation. God guards. And what seems impossible, with God's care, is *not* impossible.

Then Jesus again touched Jahmai's leg. Jahmai could feel a warmth in his touch, in the gentle, caring touch. Jesus' hand held the leg, pressing it now, pressing it and lifting it so that Jahmai found himself standing taller. He did not look down, but kept his eye fixed upon Jesus. Jesus now stood, taking his hand from the twisted leg he placed both hands upon the arms of Jahmai, ever lifting him, straightening him, pulling him up, up, up.

Finally he said, "Jahmai, you are well!" His words were not now in the warm and homey conversation. His words were with command. He was speaking an order. "Jahmai, stand before God. Even as your name, Jahmai, God guards you. Be whole in that special care!"

Somehow Jahmai knew that Jesus was talking of more than his leg. With a quick glance downward he could still see the bend in the knee — but maybe not as much. "Jahmai," Jesus continued, still holding his shoulders up, "your Heavenly Father has love for you that makes you complete, whole, that guards you well." Some of the folks nearby gave out a cry, for they had never seen Jahmai stand so tall, never hold his head so erect. "It is a miracle," they said to one another. "It is another miracle."

I WILL LEAVE THE STORY somewhat vague, for the mists of two thousand years are hard to penetrate. There were some that day who said that Jahmai's leg was straightened out just like your leg and mine. "It happened just like that," they reported with snapping fingers. Others said that Jahmai was certainly different in the way he walked, and he never was last one again — although it was still difficult for him to be the first, what with all the younger children who had run all their lives.

And what did Jahmai think? He was certain that his walking improved, and that those within the village improved in their appreciation of him. He was no longer relegated to the women's work of net-mending. He was given a man's work, tying the boats to the trees that dotted the shore line.

The wholeness that came that day from Jesus had more to do with who Jahmai *was* than with what Jahmai *had* — or did not have. The gospel message was of worth in God's sight. In that special moment his leg was less important than it had been all his fourteen years. In that special moment, Jahmai was important — named with meaning, tied in lineage to the people. And the village sensed it, too, seeing the little cripple as a person of individual worth.

Wholeness, completeness, comes into life with such understanding. It can be a resurrection! It *is* a resurrection! The badly twisted cripple or the most glamorous cinema star is partial if only body is considered. A twisted mind can make for half a human more easily than a twisted leg.

Miracles still happen! For the word of Christ Jesus, spoken today, changes partial and broken lives to whole lives. We see it as we concentrate on more than physical life. We see it as we understand that abundant life — for which Jesus gave his physical life — contains a spirit heartbeat. It is the spirit heartbeat of resurrected lives in the care of God. And that really is the story of your life.

Worship Aids for Easter 6

Call to Worship
The Lord is my light and my salvation . . . as the Psalmist attests to faith, so we, by our presence this hour, proclaim our faith and seek the guiding of God's Holy Spirit. Here, in this hour and within this fellowship, God is our light and God is our salvation. (Psalm 27)

Opening Prayer
   Beyond the sea is Galilee
      And ways which Jesus trod,
   And hidden there are those high hills
      Where He communed with God;
   Yet on the plains of common life,
      Through all the world of men,
   The voice that once said, "Follow me,"
      Speaks to our hearts again.*

Hymn Response
   "Come, Thou Long-expected Jesus" (v. 1)

Continuing Prayer
   O Life that seems so long ago,
      And yet is ever new,
   The fellowship of love with Thee,
      Through all the years is true.
   O Master over death and time,
      Reveal Thyself, we pray,
   And as before amongst Thine own,
      Dwell Thou in us today.*

Hymn Response
   "Come, Thou Long-expected Jesus" (v. 2)

Pastoral Prayer
   Holy and Eternal God, in the heritage of Bible faith we are gathered to worship, to praise, to confess, to resolve. With guidance

---

*W. Russell Bowie, *Christ in Poetry*, edited by Thomas Curtis Clark, Association Press, New York City, 1952.

of your Spirit we can leave this place of sacred meeting better able to deal with the daily life before us.

Our praise is for your gifts of goodness; gifts that provide the care and nurture in life. We are blessed beyond so many others in this world. We are not deprived of food. We are not denied shelter. Nor are we chained to someone else's thoughts. We are free. How blessed we are. How fortunate. For this we prayfully speak our thanksgiving and praise.

And we confess. Your intentions for life have been thwarted by our sometime lack of interest, lack of daring, lack of perception. Our comforts too often insulate us from the pained and imprisoned and impoverished. We confess a Christian anemia. We have heard the words of Jesus, "to the least of these, my brethren." Yet, as Jesus was too well known to us. We are so comfortable as to be untouched by almost every discomfort in the world. Yet, a discomfort within leads to confession.

So from confession it is an offering of self that we would make this day. An offering of mind and will, an offering of speech and deed, an offering of self that will move us from boring mediocrity and churchiness to the exciting uncertainty of discipleship.

We pray for your presence: in the spirit of this hour, in the words spoken, in the minds that hear, in the music, in the emotion of Christian commitments that will move us from this place changed, renewed, empowered, because You have been here... and because we respond to Your presence. Amen

Benediction

And the Psalmist wrote, The Lord is the stronghold of life; of whom shall I be afraid? Go out into the world in that faith, holding to the strengths of God's spirit in all that you do. And do not be afraid. God is love and you are loved. Amen

Study Suggestions for Chapter Six

Group Builder

Jahmai's name came from a great man and meant, "God guards." Ask each person the significance of his or her name. (Examples: My first name was one my Mother liked, My middle name comes from my grandfather, or My last name is German and means "Field-farmer.")

Discussion Questions

1. The author implies that Jahmai's leg was crippled by his delivery at birth, yet his mother "simply raised her eyes heavenward" when asked why. Is suffering which is caused by human error or ignorance God's will?

2. What was the relationship between Jahmai's physical handicap and his self-image?

3. Why do you think Jesus insisted on talking to Jahmai about the meaning of his name and about the nature of faith before making him whole?

4. Jesus would often say to those He healed, "Your faith has made you whole." What kind of faith did Jahmai bring to his encounter with Jesus?

5. The author says that Jahmai knew of people Jesus had healed. Do you think that the personal testimonies of people that have been helped in some miraculous way by Christ strengthened the faith of others? What kind of testimonies are particularly effective or ineffective in doing so?

6. What do you think Jesus healed in Jahmai? How can the family, friends, and church community help with the spiritual healing of the handicapped and seriously ill?

7. In the conclusion, the author alludes to Christ's promise of abundant life. What does this promise mean to you?

Chapter Seven

Resurrection: From Slave to Child

Galatians 4:1-9

So often a road is built upon the back of an earlier pathway — one upon the other, built up and strengthened by what went before. The busy Detroit Avenue before our church (Lakewood, Ohio) was once a Pony Express route, carrying mail toward Detroit City in Michigan. That route was earlier an Indian trail through forest lands.

So it was with the road that came from Bethany, climbed across to the Mount of Olives, snaked down into the Kidron Valley, moved through the region of the Garden of Gethsemane and finally made a steep climb to the Compassion Gate of Jerusalem. That road's history went back before David's choice of Jerusalem for his temple-building, back to when Ornan discovered a smooth rock surface on the hilltop that became his grain threshing floor (2 Samuel 24). Since that first use, the road from the east into Jerusalem had been packed down with the feet of many travelers. This was the road that trade caravans had taken, bringing precious cargoes from distant lands, and bringing salt from the warm and humid depths of the Dead Sea. This was the road of the Good Samaritan story, the road from Jerusalem to Jericho. This was also the very real road of the Palm Sunday event that brought Jesus into the Holy City (Luke 19:28-48).

See it in imagination: The early morning rain was still puddled here and there, and the steamy-wet stones at the top of walls were drying under that intense Palestinian sun. It does not rain much on Jerusalem, but this morning (in imagination), as the business of a new week was beginning, everything was drenched. The rain had come in one big downpour, filling the throughs and overflowing the little patchy gardens. It turned the hardpacked road into a slippery path. But as quickly as it had come it had ended. Now the sun was completing the clean up.

In the midst of that clean up, that drying out, the pilgrims moved along the road leading to the great city walls. Amid the pilgrims were the merchants, hurrying along with their wares, ready to begin the Passover holiday business.

Coming from the eastern village of Bethany was the happiest band of pilgrims to ever approach Jerusalem. Their leader rode a beautiful white donkey, whose nodding head marked each step of the way. The pilgrims sang the songs of David. They danced along the road even as David had danced before the Lord. They flayed the air with palm branches. Riding that white donkey was Jesus. He was welcomed along the way from Bethany. Every stone's throw distance he stopped to talk with the people. His route had been heralded earlier. Now the crowds that had so eagerly sought his teaching and healing in the Galilee shouted out their joy with his arriving at the gate of Jerusalem.

The donkey, with its special cargo, slowed during the final ascent to the city. The road pitched higher. The crowds were greater. The branches were wildly waved. The individual shouts were now blended into choruses of the Psalms: "Hozanna! Blessed is he who comes in the name of the Lord! (Psalm 118:26).

In the final distance before the great arch of the gate, the palms were laid down upon the still-wet road. Even cloaks were strewn upon the way that the donkey might have a special carpet, a royal carpet, upon which to walk. "Hozanna," the people sang. "Praise God!"

Jesus was entering the Holy City, acclaimed by many

people as their saviour. "Jesus," they said to one another, "is the special gift from God. Messiah!"

Jesus' disciples, having walked with him the whole way from Galilee, were caught up in the acclaim, sharing in the shouting and exuberance. This was *their* Master, *their* teacher. He was being ushered into the Great City even as would be a king!

The journey that Jesus took that first Palm Sunday illustrates the Biblical call to move from slavery to being sons and daughters of God. Earlier, the disciples had urged Jesus' retreat to the safety of Galilee. There the leaders were fewer and less hostile. But in Jerusalem he faced increased tension, trouble, torture — and even death.

Yet, Jesus did not retreat. His response to the proposal was, "Get behind me, Satan!" Jesus' power was a steadfastness to God's purposes, God's will, God's intention. His Heavenly Father would be his strength — his only strength if that be the case. He was in lineage to his Heavenly Father. He would not be slave to his fear, slave to his followers' fears, slave to any lesser influence in life. Jesus would be a true son of his Heavenly Father, and so he rode the little donkey along the ancient road, coming at last to the gate of the city. And he entered.

There were other roads in that ancient time, built upon earlier trails that went from place to place. One such road was from Jerusalem to Damascus. Today it is the road from the lead city of Israel to the capital of Syria. It is a raod through rugged hill landscapes as well as beautiful and lush valleys.

Upon that road, not so many years after Jesus' entry to Jerusalem, a fanatical Jew walked. Within his robes he held a decree that allowed him to arrest any Christian he could find. The purity of the Hebrew faith was at stake, he believed. Saul could see it so clearly — in simple black and white terms. "Either the Christians are liquidated, or the religion of Abraham will be doomed." The fire in Saul's eye was matched by the fire in the sun's hot rays as he marched the road from

Jerusalem to Damascus.

Upon that road he was stopped dead in his tracks, blinded by the sun in the sky and by a spirit that rested upon his soul. "Saul, why do you persecute me!" (Acts 21:6-11) The voice of Jesus echoed, if not from the distant hills, at least from the inner recesses of Saul's conscience. Lying flat against the roadbed, Saul was converted — and in that conversion he was adopted by God in a way that changed him from slave to son.

It even changed his name — from Saul to the Paul. Roman citizenship, inherited from his earthly father, allowed him access to all the roads of the empire. He took speedy gait upon them, and became the first missionary of the freedom-faith of Christ, proclaiming Jesus as *his* Lord and Saviour.

Sometimes the travel was easy, in companionship with Timothy and Gaius and Barnabas and John Mark. Sometimes it was hard travel, chased by angry and violent opponents. Sometimes the travel was with dragging chains as he was prisoner for the faith he now claimed. Yet, on he went. Paul was now part of the family, in link with Christ, with a claim to a Heavenly Father who claimed him.

In that union Paul wrote back to the Christians he knew in the region of Galatia — a number of communities, each holding a handful of faithful ones who knew that tie, that loving, supportive tie with God and God's son Jesus. Paul wrote back about the relationship begun on the road toward Damascus:

> *God sent forth his Son . . . so that we might receive adoption as sons. And because you are sons, God has sent the Spirit of his Son into our hearts . . . Through God you are no longer a slave but a son . . .*
>
> *(Galatians 4:6)*

Until his roadway experience, Paul saw life in terms of slavery — bound to rules of ritual, shackled to histories that separated people. The hard distinctions of Judiasm had formed a slavery just as surely as the chains and whips of Roman soldiers enslaved. Slavery was upon everyone, whether the chains were real ones of iron or whether they were spiritual ones of nationality, religious caste, sex, poverty, ignorance.

Saul the slave, now Paul the son shared that freedom faith. He worked the roads of the ancient world, traveling on his Roman citizenship. He wrote letters of support and enlightenment that were carried by runners upon those ancient roads. Those letters were held as spiritual treasures by those who received them, and eventually they were bound into the New Testament that is our own scriptures.

There are other — more modern — roads upon which God's adoption of us through Christ Jesus has been illustrated.

One was a Montgomery, Alabama road. On December 1, 1955, Rosa Parks refused to give up her seat on a public bus so that a white man might be seated. Mrs. Parks is black. She told the white bus driver that she was tired and chose to remain seated. It was the same driver who, twelve years earlier, had put her off a public bus because she would not obey his direction to pay the fare through the front door, then get off the bus in order to enter it again through the back door. Now, this driver had her arrested because she would not give up her seat for a white man. On that street in Montgomery, Alabama, the degredation of racial prejudice was changed by her act of defiance, changed in a civil rights movement that could mean freedom. Rosa Parks knew the message of the Bible that speaks to enslaved people of any age, and says, "God wills you to be free, to be sons and daughters, not slaves." That was 1955.

Ten years later, there was the 54-mile road between Montgomery and Selma. Upon that road on March 3, 1965, two-thousand persons marched to dramtize the injustice of voting rights denied black people. When those marchers reached the apex of the Pettus Bridge, they were greeted by club-swinging law officers, tear-gas barrages and snarling police dogs. Through the unblinkng eye of a television camera the world saw close up the beatings and the bitings. That "Bloody Sunday" became the turning point in the civil rights movement begun by Rosa Parks' action. It moved the Congress of our nation to pass the Voting Rights Act.

Behind it all was a religious conscience, and the leadership of Dr. Martin Luther King, Jr. for a non-violent process of public demonstration. But behind that leadership was the Gospel of Jesus Christ, holding up the worth of every individual in the sight of God — every individual. They knew the Bible message. "You are *not* a slave, God claims you for a son, a daughter."

And we hear the echoes of our past anguish coming today from the roads of South Africa. The Bible message, the message of God in Christ, does not overlook the slavery of apartheid. There is a clear understanding of the Bible's message. It *is* a "liberation theology" to any people in slavery. Why else would the Bible be outlawed in parts of Russia and communist states today?

The Bible message is that God does not want you enslaved. God wants you free. You are adopted, a son, a daughter. It is a resurrection message — one that we believe and share.

Jesus did not succumb to the easy way of retreating back to Galilee — back to where the pressure was less, and the pain absent, back to where the comfort could enslave him.

Paul did not take the easy way of doing his rituals within the increasing confines of an introspective Judaism and an oppressive Rome. He already knew that slavery. He claimed sonship.

Rosa Parks did not give up her bus seat to a white man because her skin was black and his was white. Rosa Parks was a daughter of God. Nor did the two thousand marchers on Pettus Bridge choose to stay home that Sunday afternoon and read the newspaper.

Today there are Christians in South Africa — white and black — who are reading their Bibles, and learning the resurrection message anew. Others in Central America are discovering in Christ power to achieve freedom from slavery that old ways have maintained. They are sons and daughters under God.

And, of course, you walk a road, too. We all do in this life. It is a road that has been walked upon by others, tracing our human story back through the centuries. The Christian call is that we dare not walk life's road as slaves — bound by whatever shackles us to being less that God intends for us. We walk it as sons and daughters, adopted by God in Christ, free to be all that God calls us to be.

Worship Aids for Easter 7

Call to Worship
"With all my heart will I praise the Lord in company of good persons, in the whole congregation. Great are the doings of the Lord; all persons study them for their delight." Here let us begin a service of praise and study, seeking God's covenenat presence. (Psalm 111)

Opening Prayer
We would see Jesus! We would look upon
The light in that divinely human face,
Where lofty majesty and tender grace
   In blended beauty shone.
We would see Jesus, and would hear again
The voice that charmed the thousands by the sea,
Spoke peace to sinners, set the captives free,
   And eased the sufferers' pain.*

Hymn Response
"We would see Jesus; lo, his star is shining" (v. 4)

Continuing Prayer
We would see Jesus, yet not him alone —
But see ourselves as in our Maker's plan;
And in the beauty of the Son of Man
   See man upon his throne.
We would see Jesus, and let him impart
The truth he came among us to reveal,
Till in the gracious message we should feel
   The beating of God's heart.*

Hymn Response
"We would see Jesus; lo, his star is shining" (v. 5)

The Pastoral Prayer
Eternal God, we are a mixed company in this place. Some of us have prayed here for many years; others of us are new — perhaps new to prayer as well as this place.

---

*W. J. Suckow, *Christ in Poetry,* edited by Thomas Curtis Clark, Association Press, New York City, 1952, p. 87.

We come with prayers of thanksgiving for the many blessing and benefits of life. Not only for our freedoms in this nation, but also for the abundance of good things showerd upon us — even as we talk of limits and scarcity and inflation. How blessed we are to be alive this day, and in this nation. Make us appreciative, O God.

We come with prayers fo petition. Your Spirit is needed upon our living. We are marked with weaknesses where strengths can be. We are stained by guilt, where the freshness of forgiveness can make the essential difference. We are limited by illness — in body, in mind — where health and fullness should be. We are in need . . . and pray for Your will and creative intention to be worked in and through us.

We also pray for others. Friends and loved ones need Your blessing. We pray for them in their particular need in the silence of this time (pause). But there are unknown persons, who are marked this day with poverty, hunger, disease, imprisonment, and selfishness. For them we pray. May they be counted into the accomplishment of Your will — and find there loving ties as children of God.

We are a mixed company, O God, but we seek to be one congregation in prayer. Amen

Benediction

"God sent and redeemed his people; God decreed that his covenant should always endure. Holy is God's name, inspiring awe. The fear of the Lord is the beginning of wisdom, and they who live by it grow in understanding." In this faithful blessing we leave now to share the Good News of the family of faith. (Psalm 111)

Study Suggestions for Chapter Seven

Group Builder

In a small group ask each person to share his or her answers to the question, "What is one freedom that you especially cherish?"

This may be a political freedom, such as freedom of speech. It may be a freedom that has been the result of discipline, such as the freedom to play the piano, or the freedom from a former bad habit. It may be a freedom that one experiences as a gift, such as freedom from pain or freedom from depression. It may be another kind of freedom that someone in your group may suggest.

Discussion Quesions

1. The author begins by describing the freedom of Jesus to enter Jerusalem on Palm Sunday despite the dangers. In what way does a concern for personal security inhibit our freedom?

2. The author continues with the story of Saul of Tarsus and his conversion on the Damascus Road. In what ways can religion enslave us?

3. The author cites the movement toward civil rights in the South and in South America. In what ways does racial prejudice limit the freedom, not only of the oppressed, but of the oppressors as well?

4. The author concludes by saying that we are called as Christians to walk life's road in freedom, not in slavery, and to help others walk it, too. "That is the *message* of Palm Sunday, but the *power* to be free — that waits for Easter." How does Easter give us the power to be free of the slavery imposed by: a) a concern for personal security, b) the bonds of false religion, c) the bonds of prejudice and hatred?

www.ingramcontent.com/pod-product-compliance
Lightning Source LLC
Chambersburg PA
CBHW071737040426
42446CB00012B/2385